D1193976

THE FIRST GENERATION

The future Hopes of this Colony depends
upon the rising Generation—Little can be
expected from the Convicts who are grown
old in vice, but much may be done for their
Children under proper Instructions.

REV. SAMUEL MARSDEN
to the Bishop of London
11 March 1821

The First Generation

SCHOOL AND SOCIETY IN EARLY AUSTRALIA

John F. Cleverley

SYDNEY UNIVERSITY PRESS

SYDNEY UNIVERSITY PRESS
Press Building, University of Sydney

Great Britain, Europe, North America
INTERNATIONAL SCHOLARLY BOOK SERVICES, INC.

First published 1971
© John F. Cleverley 1971
Library of Congress Catalog Card Number 72-166084
National Library of Australia registry card number and
ISBN 0 424 06230 5 cloth bound edition
ISBN 0 424 06250 X paper bound edition

This book is supported by money from
THE ELEANOR SOPHIA WOOD BEQUEST

Printed in Australia at The Griffin Press, Adelaide
and registered in Australia for transmission by post as a book

CONTENTS

PREFACE

A remarkable feature of life in the penal settlement of New South Wales was the exertion of colonists in fostering the education and welfare of the first generation of Australians. After just three years of settlement, schools supported by the government had opened in the townships of Sydney and Parramatta and at the sister settlement of Norfolk Island. The rapid, vigorous growth of education was the result of circumstances which saw the educational thought of the old world modified by the exigencies of a convict colony and its outcome was a system uniquely Australian.

The period from 1788 to 1809 demonstrated the urgent concern of colonists with government sponsored and private education. It revealed tensions between state, church and dissent, saw the introduction of welfare services for destitute children, brought efforts to master basic teaching techniques, and produced attempts to transform the children of the Aborigines. A measure of the priority colonists gave to education in their thinking was evident when they readily divested themselves of English precedents in schooling both for the sake of their own children and for the future. The significance of their endeavours could be minimized if the habits of these early years had been discarded. However, practices like the resort to the government for land, buildings, school supplies and teachers, and the conscious fashioning of a truly public education, became part of a continuous tradition in Australian education which was to outlast the convict era.

The purpose of this study is to identify colonial education *ab initio*; as well as to argue its significance for the years ahead. Because any examination of schooling must necessarily reveal much of society, so the working out of colonists' plans for the children of the settlement provides its own perspective on the contemporary scene. This may well be at variance with evidence from more visible sources. It is hoped that by telling the story of education in the early years of the foundation of Australia, a contribution will be made to a better understanding of the works of the men and women who came to make their homes in a new land at the turn of the nineteenth century.

I am grateful to the staffs of the Public Record Office, the Mitchell Library and the New South Wales State Archives for their helpfulness and for permission to quote from their holdings. I am also indebted to the many workers whose research has assisted my studies. In particular I wish to thank Dr C. Turney for access to his unpublished research; Mr R. F. Doust, Senior Archivist of the Archives Authority of New South Wales, for his generally invaluable assistance; Professor R. Selby Smith for his encouragement of the project; and Mrs J. Anderson, Mrs E. Wilson and Mrs F. Maslen. I especially wish to thank my wife.

J.F.C.

Chapter I

THE DEMAND FOR EDUCATION IN THE PENAL SETTLEMENT OF NEW SOUTH WALES

> Train up a child in the way he should go:
> and when he is old, he will not depart from
> it.
>
> PROVERBS, 22.6

When the six transports and three storeships of the First Fleet, guarded by the Royal Navy escorts H.M.S. *Sirius* and *Supply*, left Spithead, England, in mid-May 1787, they had aboard Governor Arthur Phillip and his small staff, a party of marines commanded by Major Robert Ross and 759 men and women convicts.[1] The Fleet with its thousand-odd community stood off Botany Bay eight months later and, on the evening of 26 January 1788, the convoy was safely at anchor in Port Jackson. Why this costly way of ridding Britain of some of her most hardened criminals was ever agreed to, has yet to be fully explained. A minority claims that it was motivated by British imperialism, others point to mercantilists' calculations of economic gain, though most argue that it was simply the surest way of emptying Britain's over-crowded gaols. While the motives behind the colony's foundation remain contentious, there can be no doubt that its daily routines were dictated by its all-pervading penal nature. Indeed it was precisely because New South Wales was a penal colony that two schools wholly supported by the government had opened by 1792 for the thirty-six children landed from the Fleet's transports.

In the hectic weeks before sailing, thoughts of a schooling for the children condemned to a Botany Bay childhood were crowded out by the more mundane priorities of fixing their food ration and clothing them. When Major Ross visited the transports loading at the Motherbank, he discovered a marine, his wife and their two children trying to keep themselves alive on a ration and a half.[2] The outraged Ross put in an official complaint to headquarters. A similar situation confronted the government official in charge of loading the *Charlotte*. He wrote to Secretary of State Evan Nepean disclosing that though he was caring for two young children whose mothers were convicts, no ration had been fixed for them by the Navy Board or for the marines' children either. The official claimed that the twenty children aboard could 'barely subsist on that Proportion they receive from their mothers' allowance'.[3] Remedial action was taken when Phillip himself took up the issue with Lord Sydney[4] who declared that such children were to be rationed at the contractors' expense.

After this direction, an order followed that the marines and convicts were to be victualled on the scale applying to soldiers serving in the West Indies. This meant a weekly ration of 7 lbs bread or flour, 7 lbs beef or 4 lbs pork, 3 pints pease, 6 ozs butter and 1 lb. flour or $\frac{1}{2}$ lb. rice as the staple adult diet.[5] The common rule-of-thumb measure applied at sea allowed a child half a woman's ration which itself was fixed at two-thirds a man's. A regulation-fed ten-year-old then could look forward to a daily helping of five hunks of bread and butter, a thick cut of salt beef, a cup of dried peas and a small damper washed down, if he was lucky, by half a pint of tea.

The next essential task for the British planners was to clothe the children. Inadvertently bundles of clothing had been left behind stacked on the wharfs, while much of the stuff landed was shoddy running threadbare after a few weeks wear. The packets of adult ready-mades contained many duplicate and wrong sizes and it was necessary to run up hessian sacks for some although a few convict

The Charge of Clothing a Boy	£	s.	d.
a Boy's Suit	0	14	0
a Shirt of Dowlas Cloth	0	2	6
a pr. Stockings	0	0	10
a Knit Cap	0	0	10
a Band	0	0	3
a pr. of Shoes	0	3	0
	£1	2s.	4d.[6]

The Charge of Clothing a Girl	£	s.	d.
a Gown and Pettycoat	0	9	6
a Coif and band of fine Ghenting	0	1	6
a Shift of Dowlas Cloth	0	2	6
a Checkered Apron	0	1	0
a pr. of Leather Stays	0	4	6
a do. Stockings	0	0	10
a do. of Shoes	0	2	6
	£1	2s.	4d.

women had managed somehow to pack a chest of finery with which to celebrate the day of the landing.[7] The decision as to the choice of the clothing for children thought suitable for the Botany Bay climate was left to the officials of the Slops Office who based their thinking on the charity school issue of the day (*see* table on p. 2).

The first replacement consignment of clothes sent by the British government was aboard the *Guardian*[8] which struck an iceberg off the Cape and fresh supplies did not reach the colony until the *Lady Juliana* berthed in 1790. She discharged 2,000 yds of Ozenberg cloth, 1,500 yds of baize, 100 small blankets, 100 pairs of small shoes and 70 hats[9] exclusively for the use of the children. Over the previous months the youngsters had to make do with what was serviceable out of the original shipment and on the quality of the running repairs their mothers had made to the new suits in which they were dressed prior to the first landing. Here they were more fortunate than their fathers some of whom were forced to labour naked in the paddocks when their clothes wore through.[10]

The first decision which originated in England directly connected with the education of the colony's children came with Phillip's Additional Instructions of 1789 whereby he was directed to allocate land in each township to support a Church of England clergyman and a schoolmaster. The relevant clause stated:

> . . . it is Our further Will and Pleasure that a particular spot in or as near each town as possible be set apart for the building of a church, and four hundred acres adjacent thereto allotted for the maintenance of a minister, and two hundred for a schoolmaster.[11]

Phillip promptly made a reservation of 1,000 acres which included a Crown block of 600 acres for a minister and a schoolmaster in the Petersham Hill district to the west of Farm Cove and fronting the harbour.[12] Most of the land was leased for private grazing but it returned no bonus for the support of schools in its unimproved state.

The policy of endowing a church with wasteland in an attempt to secure the future of religion and education was not unique to New South Wales. Many years before the British settled Canada, the French had applied an identical policy there to alienate vast estates for the Jesuits for religious and educational purposes and Church of England glebes had been allowed in Nova Scotia in 1749.[13] More Church of England land endowments in North America followed and the presence of Empire Loyalists in the maritime states in 1786 had brought the suggestion that 'Two or three thousand Acres set apart for a Glebe, and the Use of a School, in every new Township or District, would lay the Foundation of a future Maintenance for Clergymen and Schoolmasters'.[14] The

ultimate step in provision of this kind came when the Colonial
Office set aside one-seventh of the lands in Upper Canada as an
exclusive endowment for the Church of England and its schools
under the Constitution Act of 1791.

Land endowment for churches and schools in New South Wales
preceded the Canadian Act by two years and was applied to Norfolk
Island in 1792 and to Van Diemen's Land in 1804. Explaining the
British government's intentions, Spencer Perceval, Chancellor of the
Exchequer in the administration of the Duke of Portland, told
Governor William Bligh: 'Such arrangements are easy in the early
state of the colony, and are impossible afterwards without a great
expence'.[15] But it was precisely this ease of alienation which
indicated a lack of demand for the land, hence its low cash return.
As schools normally require an immediate income, the government's
foresight was of very limited usefulness when it came to supporting
colonial education.

While Britain took some account of the physical welfare of the
colony's children and through the alienation of Crown land had
made a gesture for their future, she did not directly initiate projects
in education for them. It could be argued that the strong prejudice
against spending public money on education which existed in
England at the time was a major reason for this position. But
English precedents were not invariably the determinants of policy
outside England. Ireland was a case in point where several thousand
pounds were spent on education annually in the unrewarding task
of attempting to transform the children of Roman Catholic peasants
into right-thinking Protestant boys and girls. It was more likely that
the organizers felt no special urgency about appointing a schoolmaster to sail with the Fleet when initially so few children were
involved and before local requirements became better known.

At this time schoolmasters were not public servants and the
planners could reasonably expect that if a demand for teachers was
felt in England, then a Church of England religious society would
meet it, as had happened in some of the North American Crown
colonies. The dictates of economy were a further consideration
which prevented the anticipation of staffing requirements too far in
advance. This was most apparent in the list of the governor's staff
which, exclusive of the offices of governor and lieutenant-governor,
comprised only eight senior and three petty officials, surely one of
the smallest establishments ever to undertake the responsibilities of
a colonial administration.

British policy on colonial education leaned heavily on local
advice, her officials mostly accepting that solutions arising from
on-the-spot assessments were best. But when the time came for

action on some of these local recommendations, British support varied considerably in its effectiveness. It was strongest where it involved the comparative ease of a cash payment, weakest when it came to the actual recruitment of teachers and the supply of textbooks. The British treasury found the money for the colony's first stone schoolhouse, also for an expensive private house in Sydney for conversion into a girls' orphanage, and its officials were prepared to let sleeping dogs lie over the question of the legality of the special taxes raised to maintain these institutions. In due course the authorities responded to requests for schoolmasters from England by including their salaries in the New South Wales estimates for 1809.

This awareness in England that education in a penal settlement required quite different means of encouragement from that given at home was apparent when governors John Hunter and Bligh were closely questioned at the Select Committee on Transportation of 1812 about the state of education in the colony. So far as New South Wales was concerned, Whitehall's policy gave *de facto* recognition to the notion that government aid for public education was justifiable. This was in marked contrast to the state of affairs in England where no government money was spent on elementary education before 1833.

Acceptance of the idea that it was appropriate for the government to foster schools in a penal colony may suggest that the English prison system maintained schools in its gaols and that these had served as models from which the colonists gleaned ideas and inspiration. But this was not the case. Indeed by the 1780s the English prison system was close to a complete breakdown. During the operation of transportation to America, English gaols had served primarily as holding centres for those awaiting trial who were then either acquitted, summarily punished, transported or executed. Long terms of imprisonment played no part in the penal code of the day. With the cessation of transportation to America, which followed the Declaration of Independence of 1776, the sheer weight of numbers upset the previous balance between the parish relief schemes and the practice of short-term commitals to gaol. Delinquents who would once have been admitted to Houses of Correction found themselves gaoled and the long-term imprisonment of debtors became commonplace. The expedient solution of hulks was introduced in an attempt to cope with these pressures. These were converted men-o'-war to which convicts were assigned to await the re-introduction of transportation.

The hulks however merely served an overflow. The *State of the Prisons* report by the Quaker reformer John Howard, depicted English gaols in the 1770s as places crammed with underfed prisoners who were incarcerated in unhygienic and unventilated cells. Sometimes acquitted prisoners were returned to prison because they could not afford their warders' dues for keeping them alive up to the date of their trial. Among the inmates Howard found a multitude of youngsters, gaoled for trifling offences, who had become totally ruined there. Worse still, many of the children in the gaols had not been committed to them. They were the children of debtors' families, some of whom were imprisoned for debts as little as £10. In 1776 the London Fleet Gaol alone housed 475 children yet it was without a surgeon or schoolmaster. As part of his reforms, Howard wanted these debtors' families removed from the gaols and the youngest of the prisoners put under a 'kind and tender monitor'.[16]

Howard's meticulous reports did not record one school in an English gaol. Not until the turn of the nineteenth century was a modest start made on prison reform when political action at long last began to mend some of the worst and most obvious abuses and new prisons were erected. By then the utilitarian philosopher, Jeremy Bentham, had drafted his revolutionary plans for a penitentiary in which rooms were specifically set aside for schoolmasters. His scheme required that the contractor hire a 'sufficient Number of competent Schoolmasters . . . by whom Instruction shall be administered on every Sunday at the least, during the Intervals of Meals and Divine Service, in Reading, Writing, and Arithmetic'.[17] One of the first prisons to mount an education programme was H.M. Cold Bath Fields Gaol whose working regulations permitted the 'more orderly' prisoners to teach young offenders to read and where both teacher and pupil were given 'an Extra-recompence, the one for learning, and the other for teaching'.[18]

By the 1800s several other English prisons had opened schools. That part of Gloucester Gaol designed as a model penitentiary contained facilities which enabled prisoners to be locked up in individual cells on Sundays with a Bible, prayer book and Melmoth's *Importance of Religion*. Its chaplain planned a Sunday school also, but had abandoned the idea when he could only recruit Methodist teachers whose religious tenets the prison governor regarded as 'unfavourable to penitence and remorse for past conduct'.[19] Instead the chaplain had to content himself with passing on spelling books to illiterate prisoners and letting 'the best informed' of the others act as instructors. It was a tribute to his perseverance and the teachers' abilities that those imprisoned for several years at Gloucester Gaol 'invariably learned to read'. The chaplain did not encourage writing or accounting lessons being of the opinion that such skills were 'totally unnecessary to their reformation'. He made one exception though of an illiterate convict committed for highway robbery and later re-sentenced for an attempted escape. The man learned to read, write and prepare accounts sufficiently well in his time at Gloucester to get a job as bailiff to a farmer in his home county. After his discharge he was to receive the county award of £3 sterling for faithful service by a reformed convict.

In the 1780s there was literally nothing that Governor Phillip could have learned about education from the English prison system which would have helped him meet the strong demand for schools which appeared very early in his governorship. This demand was based on the special role education was thought to have in a penal settlement and on the rapid increase in the child population. Certainly the organizers of the venture had been astray in thinking in terms of a slow initial population growth. The thirty-six children who disembarked from the Fleet were joined by another eleven from the *Lady Juliana* in June 1790.* In all around twenty-two children had joined the Second Fleet and about a dozen disembarked from the Third Fleet in 1791.[20] By 1801 just on one hundred children had accompanied the six thousand-odd convicts who were transported to New South Wales.[21]

But more significant than the number of children who came to the colony aboard the convict transports was the natural increase in a society where the men outnumbered the women (most of whom were of child-bearing age) by over three to one, and where the women could be expected to be at least as fertile as their sisters at home who, on an average, had a child every two years between the ages of twenty and forty.[22] By early 1790, with births exceeding deaths, the children of convicts numbered twenty-three in Sydney and thirty-seven on Norfolk Island exclusive of the officers' children.[23] By the close of 1792 there were about 246 children in the colony[24] almost equally divided between the mainland and Norfolk Island. These figures were exclusive of the child convicts a few of whom had been transported as young as twelve years of age.[25]

Many of these child prisoners were drawn from the cities.[26] Some began as 'cadgers' at six years of age, were seasoned pickpockets with criminal records by twelve, and unless transported young could expect to be hanged before their majority. A tender age was not by itself any guarantee of immunity from transportation or a capital sentence. In April 1788, a youth in his teens was one of the first executed in the colony.[27] Nevertheless it was uncommon to find children under fifteen transported, although some offenders fifteen

---

* Child population figures used throughout are not as accurate as the numerical estimates imply. Musters and counting procedures were generally imperfect.

and above were given the sentence in the belief that it would give them a chance in life by keeping them out of the unspeakable prisons. Lacking suitable employment, deserted by their parents and running in child-gangs, many of these delinquent errand boys, stable hands and servants had learned the refinements of their preferred crimes in gaol, and had come to prefer a comradeship outside the law above the advantages of an honest sixteen-hour working day. Probably it was these youngsters who gained most from a sentence to Botany Bay even if their rehabilitation was very much of a lottery. No organized attempt was undertaken to make them literate or to teach them a useful trade until Macquarie opened his Barracks and before schools on shipboard became common in the 1830s.

To the casual observer, youngsters appeared to be everywhere in the colony but their numbers alone were no guarantee that schools would open for them. In contemporary Western society more children were outside schools than were in them. Rather it was the failure of the establishment to turn individual convicts into good citizens which was to have the greater influence, albeit an indirect one. In a public address after the landing, Phillip proclaimed that social discipline would be his first priority and he promised the convicts that 'the industrious sh'd not labour for the idle; if they did not work they sh'd not eat'.[28] Not all his listeners responded. A few thought little enough of their prospects to abscond, while others hid their working tools, or by acts of petty thieving preyed on their fellows. The naked coercion of the state appeared a fortnight later when the first session of the Court of Criminal Judicature directed a severe flogging and another man was ordered into solitary confinement on a small island in the harbour. Within the space of a month a man had been hanged.[29] Discipline imposed from the top often proved ineffectual but, paradoxically, its failure was especially important in encouraging the opening of schools as it prompted the governing *élite* to think in terms of the next generation.

Many influential colonists appear to have held the opinion that the convict population was incapable of genuine rehabilitation. Here they shared in the pessimism of most contemporary thinkers. Only a minority of penologists was on record for having considered otherwise, the best known of whom was Jeremy Bentham who had included the notion of reform in the aims of his model prison, the Panopticon. Bentham had been an alert observer of the various English parish relief schemes with their pretentious claim that sturdy beggars could be transformed through hard labour into industrious ratepayers. It was the abject failure of these Houses of Correction and Bridewells, run as they mostly were for the private profit of the contractors who made their livings from screwing the paupers, the infirm and the unemployed, which had opened the way for the schemes of the systematic social reformers. These men were sufficiently realistic to link reform and employment together. Bentham wanted existing welfare institutions shut down and replaced by proper industrial schools capable of instructing their inmates 'in the most useful Branches of vulgar learning, as well as in some Trade or Occupation'.[30]

However, spokesmen for social reform made little headway in England until after the end of the Napoleonic wars when their efforts were seconded by the socially-conscious evangelicals who started to press hard for state subsidies for their improvement programmes. By then the feasibility of reformation had become an essential ingredient in the metaphysics of Wilberforce's conversions; it had encouraged Hannah More in her forays among the unconverted, poverty-stricken Welsh miners; and had added substance to Methodists' dreams of universal adult salvation.

The generation which had organized the Fleet were essentially realists who had little time for speculations like reform when they put forward their pragmatic arguments on the best sites of exile for convicts ranging from Nova Scotia, south to the Floridas and the West Indies, and eastwards to Yanimarew, 400 miles up the river Gambia on the West Coast of Africa. Admittedly the earliest convict shippings to Maryland had made obeisance to the possibility of reform in that they depended on the prisoners' consent to contract their labour to the plantation owners in return for a pardon which, in theory at least, gave them a chance to start afresh. But by the time the second era of transportation began to clear the hulks in 1787, the intention of reform was an irrelevant issue when the authorities weighed the advantages expected to follow from purging the country of its criminal element.[31]

Nor did the objective of reform appear to have inspired the efforts of many of the paid officials who directed the daily lives of the convicts in the gaols and aboard the hulks. The full force of the reasons behind their disenchantment came home to the Fleet's chaplain, Rev. Richard Johnson, long before he had actually experienced life in the penal settlement. In October 1786, Johnson's churchmen sponsors had him aboard the prison hulk *Leviathan* moored at Woolwich where he was given the opportunity to meet face-to-face 250 of his future congregation. The encounter proved abortive for both convicts and clergymen except in so far as it challenged notions Johnson may have had of easy conversions or even of expecting thanks for his efforts. The chaplain did not seek out convicts again until he was required to embark on the *Charlotte* in March 1787.[32]

From his experiences in the colony, Johnson deduced that it was hopeless to expect convicts to change their ways and he came to accept the point of view that the future must be with the colony's children. However he did not come to this conclusion without much soul-searching. As late as his third year, he was anticipating that 'in time, in spight of all opposition & obstacles, God will make bare his holy arm in the Conversion & salvation of the Souls of men'.[33] And in 1792 he wrote home to a friend in England asking him to recruit someone prepared to establish schools on Sundays for illiterate convicts in New South Wales with the intention of bringing 'some of these unhappy wretches to a better way of thinking'.[34] Johnson took this opportunity to re-affirm that his ardent wish was to witness 'the Reformation of these miserable & deluded people'.[35] But by 1794 Johnson had shifted his ground. He was admitting privately that 'If any Hopes are to be formed of any Reformation being effected in this Colony, I believe it must begin amongst those of the rising generation'.[36]

Further weight was added to Johnson's argument by the views of the Rev. Samuel Marsden who declared, after only a short residence in the colony, that 'the only prospect of a minister's usefulness is in the rising generation'.[37] The assistant chaplain thought it self-evident that there was 'little prospect of any reformation amongst the prisoners at large'.[38] From the widespread acceptance that religious endeavour among convicts was largely an unprofitable business, it followed that the recruitment of colonial schoolmasters, 'this article of ye first necessity',[39] was rated by the practical as a more obvious and worthwhile cause than the engagement of extra clergy. This helps explain why those who otherwise had no time for religion were fully prepared to make personal sacrifices to open schools.

Colonists who subscribed to the rising generation theory also accepted its corollary that it was possible for children to grow up as good men and women despite the corrosive environment of a penal settlement if they were given the right kind of education. A rationale for this had appeared in the writings of the seventeenth-century English philosopher, John Locke, when he stressed the educability of the child while popularizing his notion that men could attain virtue and a true idea of God through a self-imposed discipline guided by reason. Over the years the permeation of Lockean ideas in England had seen the belief in the effectiveness of environmental learning become commonplace and respectable. Certainly Locke had taken some account of heredity in his assertion that 'God has stamped certain characters upon men's minds, which like their shapes, may perhaps be a little mended, but can hardly be totally altered',[40] but his chief claim nonetheless, 'that of all the men we meet with, nine parts of ten are what they are, good or evil, useful or not, by their education',[41] was overwhelmingly on the side of the formative powers of deliberate education.

Locke conceived that the mind was analogous to 'white paper or wax to be moulded and fashioned as one pleases'.[42] And he argued that by habituation and resort to the pleasure/pain principle underlying human conduct, children could be made into moral adults. Locke's empiricism with its faith in the ultimate perfectibility of man was taken a step further by the utilitarian thinkers of the eighteenth century whose 'greatest happiness' proposition explained to the public how acts were morally justifiable. These ideas were taken up by the reformist evangelicals along with the Lockean premise that learning should always be subordinate to virtue. By the turn of the nineteenth century such viewpoints had coincided to form the basis of a powerful British lobby which propagated the religious and social utility of schools.

The last of the major arguments to aid the cause of colonial education portrayed its schools and orphanages as places where the innocent child could be effectively separated from his vicious parents. George Howe, the editor of *The Sydney Gazette*, claimed that immoral parents infected their offspring with their own iniquitous habits 'for, as a child imbibes in youth the manners of its parent, if these manners be corrupt, so also will be those of their posterity'.[43] This argument which attributed 'the growing national sins'[44] to a delinquent youth exposed to 'all the vices of their abandoned parents', found a ready audience in the colony. Influential colonists became convinced that, unless action was taken quickly, colonial children could not escape inheriting 'their abandoned parents' profligate infamy'.[45] One obvious solution was a period of quarantine in an educational institution where the native born would have 'their propensities to evil corrected, and that turn given to their attainments which should secure them a stock of useful knowledge'.[46]

Nevertheless the argument which continued in most frequent use by educationally-minded colonists and their English backers remained that based on schooling the rising generation. In 1805 Lord Castlereagh was doing more than stating what had become the accepted wisdom of his day when he advised Bligh:

> In a Settlement, where the irregular and immoral habits of the Parents are likely to leave their Children in a state peculiarly exposed to suffer from similar vices, you will feel the peculiar necessity that the Government should interfere on behalf of the rising generation and by the exertion of authority as well as of encouragement, endeavour to educate them in religious as well as industrious habits—it is reasonable that the more wealthy Inhabitants should bear the charge of educating their own

Children; but it is His Majesty's gracious Direction that the Expence, indispensably required to give effect to this interesting object, should not be withheld from the Public Funds and you are authorized to make such advances upon this account as you may deem requisite to afford the means of education to the Children of the Colony.[47]

Acceptance of the rising generation idea in England can be documented from as far back as 1795 when the Church of England Society for the Propagation of the Gospel in Foreign Parts had recorded the opinion in its minutes that 'the most likely means of effecting a reformation must be by paying all the attention that can be to the instruction and morals of the rising generation'.[48]

At the time the secretary of the SPG was preparing his records, some Englishmen were visualizing their recent colonial possession as an immense penitentiary, an institution in which free men and convicts were equally cogs in a machine designed to serve the functions of a latter-day inferno. Although this analogy was a product of the imagination not a description of reality, it did suggest that the children of the colony would have a niche of their own and that they would not be permitted to grow up untamed, irreligious and potentially destructive outside the system. Whatever particular reason was advanced to further the cause of colonial education in England and in New South Wales, it depended for its persuasiveness on the penal environment. With the hopes of the colonists set on the next generation, schools were soon high on the list of the colony's most urgent priorities; and the decision to open them was taken possibly as early as 1789 and certainly by 1792.

Chapter II

MODELS FOR COLONIAL SCHOOLS

To every class we have a school assign'd,
Rules for all ranks and food for every mind.

G. CRABBE

The sudden, unforeseen demand for education in New South Wales forced the colonists to consider as a matter of urgency precisely what kinds of schools they wanted. A variety of ideas were available to them from English practice. Institutions there ranged from the orthodox Latin grammars, military, mathematical and commercial schools to a network of dame schools and a number of charity schools for the children of the pauper class. A few academies were also available to fee-paying parents where schoolmasters experimented with self-government and the abolition of corporal punishment, and which taught subjects like political economy and the religions of the world. However, none of these schools could be translated to a penal colony without drastic modification. In their search for suitable schools, colonists were forced to devise models of their own. These were based on their knowledge and experience of education in the Western tradition, and on the fact that the earliest schools would cater substantially for the children of the lower classes. Like all other colonial activities, their products were subject to the pressures and exigencies of life in the settlement.

Educational thought in Western Europe was in a state of ferment at the end of the eighteenth century. The old ideal of an education in the humanities, with its Christian-Platonic harmony of physical and mental states and its emphasis on the development of rational thought through the study of classical languages, had broken down in practice. The teaching of the classics had degenerated to become the mere construing of passages selected for their difficulty, while the appreciation of classical poetry had turned into the mechanics of verse construction according to the dictates of some inflexible metre. By the 1790s the old truths of a good education no longer satisfied. Unquestionably the most important source of new ideas about education was the writing of the erratic Swiss genius, Jean Jacques

13

Rousseau, whose reputation in education was based on his didactic novel *Émile* published in 1762. At the time of the colony's foundation, his slogans that education is 'nothing else but the course of nature' and that 'the first impulses of nature are always right'[1] were reverberating throughout European pedagogy.

In *Émile*, Rousseau advocated a 'negative' education designed to protect the child from the corrupt society about him, one based on the developmental stages of nature which required that the training of the faculty of reason be left until late adolescence. Most masters, he claimed, 'are always looking for the man in the child', hence their teaching relied on 'words, words, words' instead of the reality of life experience. 'Nature would have them children before they are men', the educational reformer argued, and his readers were instructed that childhood had 'its own ways of seeing, thinking, and feeling'. Rousseau's theories had no place for 'human authority' or 'the prejudices of our native land'. The author wanted the child's faith entrusted to 'the light of reason alone, in a state of nature', and, at an appropriate time, the youngster was to choose a religion to suit himself. Like Locke before him, Rousseau was unable to resist putting into his books numerous stories and helpful hints from European folk-lore on the best methods of child-rearing: from not wrapping up babies too tightly, to the advantages of youthful aristo-crats learning a manual trade. Above all else though, the Swiss prophet's disciplines were urged to trust to their emotions and to 'love childhood, indulge its sports, its pleasures, its delighful instincts'.

Aided by the publicity from a public burning in France, *Émile* had an instant success to become the most widely-read text on education since the Republic. Copybook *Émiles* sprang up all over Europe. At Dessau in north Germany, J. Basedow made a serious attempt to relate the master's theories to classroom practice. In his short-lived Philanthropinum, the schoolmaster pioneered the conver-sational method of language teaching, introduced science and nature lessons, and taught a form of religious instruction free of 'theologizing distinctions'.[2] Another more lasting exponent of the new education was Pestalozzi whose novel, *Leonard and Gertrude* published in 1781, was part of his plan to teach beggars to live like men by presenting them with the revelation of the liberating power of a natural education. As with Basedow, who had christened his daughter Émilie, the warmest of tributes from Pestalozzi to Rousseau came with the naming of his child, Jean Jacques. But while Pestalozzi was to carry Rousseau's romantic naturalism into a new century and, in time, into the schoolroom, his ideas were not popularly disseminated in England and thence to the colony until well into the 1800s.

It would be fair to say that continental ideas at the turn of the nineteenth century had attracted only a small band of ardent Rousseauphiles in England, men and women like the Edgeworths, Mary Wollstonecraft, Erasmus Darwin, Charles Lamb and William Hazlitt. Some were to take Rousseau's dictums literally and his writing encouraged a number of near-disastrous experiments in child-study where children of thirteen were brought up unable to read or write. Madame Pestalozzi was forced to teach her son secretly and Richard Edgeworth attempted a natural education on his lad but had to pack him off to boarding school in an attempt to repair the damage.

Another challenge to the traditional ways of looking at education came from some English evangelicals who disseminated educational ideas quite the contrary of Rousseau's, namely, that 'The bias of nature is set the wrong way: Education is destined to set it right'.[3] John Wesley's ideas on education were an extension of his mother's. Susannah Wesley had brought up her numerous family on the precept that their natures were sinful and that they could only be restrained by exhortation, prayer and vigorous correction. The founder of Methodism advised his followers to accept similar guide-lines:

> Break their wills betimes, begin this work before they can run alone, before they can speak plain, perhaps before they can speak at all. Whatever pains it costs, break the will, if you would not damn the child. Let a child from a year old be taught to fear the rod and to cry softly; from that age make him do as he is bid, if you whip him ten times running to effect it. If you spare the rod, you spoil the child: if you do not conquer, you ruin him. Break his will now, and his soul shall live, and he will probably bless you to all eternity.[4]

Wesley did not hold to his views in ignorance of what Rousseau had written about education either. He had read *Émile* early in 1770 and had been sufficiently impressed to jot down his reactions in his day journal:

> Sure a more consummate coxcomb never saw the sun! . . . he is a mere misanthrope; a cynic all over. So indeed is his brother-infidel, Voltaire; and wellnigh as great a coxcomb. But he hides both his doggedness and vanity a little better; whereas here it stares us in the face continually. As to his book, it is whimsical to the last degree; grounded neither upon reason nor experience. To cite particular passages would be endless; but anyone may observe concerning the whole, the advices which are good are trite and common, only disguised under new expressions. And those which are new, which are really his own, are lighter than vanity itself. Such discoveries I always expect from those who are too wise to believe their Bibles.[5]

Wesley's idea of a good school is detailed in his regulations for a girls' boarding school. The girls were to be brought up 'in the Fear of GOD: And at the utmost Distance as from Vice in general, so in particular from Idleness & Effeminacy'.[6] The school's prospectus curtly warned off any faint-hearts from requesting the enrolment of their children: 'The children therefore of tender Parents so call'd, (who are indeed offering up their Sons and Daughters unto Devils) have no Business here.' The routine of each school day was rigidly prescribed. The girls rose at four a.m. winter and summer, spent an hour in religious exercises and then at self-examination. At five they attended public worship and from six on they worked at their books until breakfast. Water only was permitted at meals and nothing was to be eaten between them. On Fridays the girls, if healthy, fasted until three in the afternoon. The school day ended at five o'clock. The children then retired for an hour of private prayer followed by a short walk before supper. A little before seven they were at public worship again and, an hour later, they were put to bed 'ye youngest first'. Wesley believed that no child should be left unsupervized and he allowed no play days. 'Neither do we allow any Time for play on any Day', he declared, 'She that plays when she is a Child, will play when she is a Woman'. The cost of all this was a reasonable £10 per annum, a sum set well within the pockets of Wesley's itinerant preachers.

While the European controversies made little impact on the local scene before the 1800s, it is likely that the educational debate was known to several of the colonial *élite*. Phillip had lived for a year in southern France; and it was probable also that the colony's surveyor, Augustus Alt, son of the one-time Ambassador for Hesse-Kassel, knew of Rousseau's work for he was a man with considerable experience of French and German life.[7] Others who could reasonably be expected to have had contact with the new ideas in education were the university-educated Johnson, a man with Methodist sympathies, and the literary-inclined Captain-Lieutenant Watkin Tench of the Marines. It would be stretching a point though to consider any members of this practically-minded *élite* as being enthusiastic converts to either continental romanticism or to the extremes of the fundamentalist doctrine of original sin. They had more in common with the majority of Englishmen who preferred an educational mixture of their own, compounded of Lockean empiricism, the wisdom of commonsense and the grateful recognition of a God-given class structure, above such extravagances as biblical scrupulosity or of leaving things to nature.

Other sources of ideas on education which were readily accessible to colonists sprang from their own schooldays and from their knowledge of educational practices overseas. The schools the *élite* attended were representative of the variety of institutions whose managers were willing to find a place for the sons of parents with a little money to invest in their children's future. For several a popular route to an education was through the ranks of the navy. Phillip, the son of a language teacher, had been enrolled at the endowed non-classical grammar school at Greenwich 'on the establishment of poor boys in the Royal Hospital for Seamen' where he was listed officially as 'a poor child',[8] one to be 'provided for and educated in the said Hospital as to make him capable of being useful in the Sea Service'. At fifteen Phillip was bound apprentice in the merchant marine but had switched to a navy career after two years. Another brought up for the sea was the commissary, John Palmer, who began his career as a captain's servant and was apparently educated from then on by the navy's schoolmasters.

Some of the *élite* were well educated by the standards of their day. The diarist, Tench, benefited from a father who ran a private-enterprise boarding-school while others had some experience of higher education. Captain John Hunter attended the University of Aberdeen briefly and the surgeon, John White, held the Diploma of the Company of Surgeons. The best qualified of all was Johnson who went from Hull Grammar School to Magdalene College, Cambridge, where he graduated Bachelor of Arts in 1784. Johnson's school at Hull had been established in the fourteenth century and was endowed later by Bishop Alcock of Worcester, a native of the town. In 1767 the bench appointed a new headmaster, Joseph Milner, a young curate from Thorpe Arch who had previously been an usher in his vicar's school. With the aid of his brother Isaac, Milner rapidly built up the school broadening its curriculum to include English grammar, mathematics and geography until it was returning above £200 per annum in fees.[9]

One of Milner's first pupils was William Wilberforce. Something of a child prodigy, Wilberforce was made to stand on the table to read aloud as an example to the other boys. However he did not remain at the school for long. In 1770 Milner was converted to 'enthusiasm' and he commenced preaching to audiences around the town

> ... as if the present probationary moments were actually the last they would have, and that if he were not listened to at that time, it might be too late ... hence his energetic descriptions of the Miseries of Sin; his awful denunciations against impenitence, and his animated exhortations to lay hold of the inestimable remedy of the Gospel.

The first fruits of Milner's conversion were the loss of some of his best scholars followed by a marked degree of social ostracism when 'few persons who wore a tolerably good coat would take notice of him when they met him in the street'.

The growing strength and respectability of the evangelical movement saw Milner rehabilitated in the 1780s and, after preaching a sermon on the mayor-making day, he was publicly thanked by the Corporation and invited to publish it. His school continued to be representative of the prosperous middle classes by presenting increasing numbers of scholars to the universities who almost invariably became clergymen; it became 'the great seminary for boys in the East Riding'. Johnson was among them, a Welton boy sent up to Cambridge in 1780. Another ex-pupil of the school was Marsden who became Johnson's assistant chaplain in 1794. Both Johnson and Marsden held to their headmaster's radical theology and were to take up strong evangelical stances in a colony whose orthodox governors regarded Methodist tendencies in Church of England clergy to be a departure from good-breeding, a sign of their adherents' low-rank and inadequate education, as well as a gross insult to themselves personally.

Another way colonists formed their ideas about education was from observations made while overseas. Evidence exists that some were keen observers of educational practices around them which differed from arrangements made at home as witnessed in Tench's and P.G. King's accounts of the orphanage at Teneriffe which they had inspected on the voyage out. For most, the common denominator of overseas experience was service in North America. Both Palmer and King had served there, Ross had spells in Canada, Phillip in Havana and White in the West Indies. Collins had lived for a time at Halifax, Nova Scotia, Tench was a prisoner of war for three months in Maryland and Hunter knew something of life in Newfoundland where the SPG had been active since 1726. The Society was responsible for sending six schoolmasters to Nova Scotia in 1749 and had six schools of its own in Newfoundland by 1790,[10] these were apart from the schools sponsored by private individuals.

Unhappily the Church of England schools in Nova Scotia did not flourish. The teacher at Halifax was sacked in 1792 for 'Drunkenness and other Irregularities'[11] and was replaced by the parish clerk, but no replacement could be found for the man at Annapolis who poisoned himself in 1768. Things improved in the small townships around Halifax in the 1760s with the migration of New England people whose communities had legislated for schools as far back as 1642. Nevertheless education did not make any substantial headway in northeast Canada generally until after the influx of the Empire Loyalists in the 1780s. Education in Upper Canada where Ross had served was even less advanced and would-be scholars were sent east to the coast or to New England if their parents wanted them educated.

In the United States proper, the variety and religious affiliations of schools were more diverse than was the case in Britain. This was not only because of the varied social backgrounds of the immigrant communities who often ran their own schools but it can also be attributed to the different modes of church-state relations. In centres like Massachusetts, the school was tied to a particular church, the Congregational, while in New Jersey and Maryland, the church-state connection at any one time depended upon the politics of the day. In other centres like Rhode Island and Delaware, a considerable degree of religious equality was already noticeable.[12] So far as elementary school administration was concerned, it ranged from the town control of New England, although by now the old puritan theocracy was declining, to a decentralized pattern of district control. By the 1780s a few political leaders had begun to canvass the idea of universal elementary education supported from public funds.

Generally speaking the movement south saw a decline in direct public involvement with the middle and southern states favouring denominational schools augmented by a system of subsidies for pauper education. However, the period after the American War of Independence was essentially one of transition in the switch from colonial to post-revolutionary thought both in regard to the popularity of certain schools, for the latin grammar was yielding its predominance to schools offering more practical studies, and in the developing concept of an elementary education for all. While there was little in the way of a consistent or new approach to elementary education which the colonists could have learned from contemporary America, a glimpse of the possible agencies which could be made responsible for its provision was there for the taking.

An important difference between the North American and the English ways of maintaining schools was the extent to which the community as a whole accepted the responsibility of ensuring that its citizens were educated in the New World, whereas the Englishman prized the right to decide for himself whether he wanted to be educated or not much too highly to countenance any interference by a paternal government or community. Already Englishmen had rejected the example of their barbarian neighbours, the Scots, who had passed The Settling of Schools Act in 1696 which required that schools open in every parish not yet provided for. Those south of the border knew better. Influential sections of the English population rejected the notion of state aid for education fearing that it would destroy religious and civil liberty. And if some continentals like La Chalotais or Turgot did advocate state intervention or were willing to argue the case for government subsidies for elementary education, and a small minority of Englishmen was found to agree with them, the British reformers were quite uncertain about how to put their programmes into practice.

The stereotype of the British attitude towards state aid for education was epitomized by Bentham who, though capable of dreaming up the Chrestomathia, or institution devoted to useful learning, was equally certain that it was a parent's right to decide for himself what was best for his own children. The social reformer had no time whatever for state control for he believed that 'the choice, the manner, and the expense of education'[13] should be left entirely to the parents. 'Every thing', Bentham argued on a point of principle, 'is advanced and developed by this emulation of individuals', and, if the state were foolish enough to intervene, 'if every thing were cast in the same mould, if instruction everywhere partook of the character of legal authority, errors would be perpetuated, and there would be no improvement'.

Other Englishmen had joined the anti-state lobby because they were scared of the possible effects if education was diffused through all social classes. Among this group was the poet, William Wordsworth. 'It is undoubtedly to be desired', Wordsworth wrote to a close friend, 'that every one should be able to read, and perhaps (for that is far from being equally apparent) to write'. However, Wordsworth was careful to remind his correspondent that one of the best and happiest men he knew was quite illiterate. 'There is too much indiscriminate gratuitous instruction in this country . . . Can it', he concluded, 'in a *general* view, be good that an infant should learn much which its *parents do not know*? Will not the child arrogate a superiority unfavourable to love and obedience?'[14]

Educational reformers and those seeking facilities for scientific training did not look to the state for money: on the contrary, they were inclined to fear state intervention for they assumed it would extend the powers of the aristocracy, the landed gentry and the Established Church. The squabbles between the bishops and their clergy, secularists and dissenters, combined with the economic advantage of child labour to keep government money out of education until the 1830s when a vote of £20,000 was allocated as bait to snare private subscriptions for the mass education societies.

Of the variety of schools in England, the dame and the charity schools had most relevance for colonial conditions when schooling for the poorer classes was under discussion. Dame schools were usually taught by barely-literate women in their own living-rooms or kitchens and the mistresses met a steady demand for the rudiments of reading in return for a small fee. For the penniless, there were always the charity schools which had been opened as far back as the sixteenth century when Edward VI and Elizabeth had directed the clergy to teach their parishioners reading and writing.

An important motive in the establishment of free schools was the religious duty of charity, a reputation for good works helping a man assure his present and future life. By the beginning of the eighteenth century, the charity school movement with its avowed aim of promoting the glory of God by extending the usefulness of man, was thriving. In return for a modest outlay, its sponsors promised society an effective antidote to ignorance, infidelity and idleness not to mention the safeguarding of the Hanoverian succession and the Protestant faith by the formation of 'little garrisons against Popery'.[15] Supported by this driving force of politics and piety and backed by a belief that its schools could improve society, an education in the charity school tradition appeared to meet some of the requirements of colonists for they too were searching for a schooling which would serve as an agency for social change.

Nevertheless there were reasons why the Anglican charity school movement could not be translated *in toto* to the colony. Its effectiveness in England had been due to support from the moneyed middle class, the organization of The Society for the Propagation of Christian Knowledge and the application of joint-stock company procedures to the founding of schools. The clergy first directed their parishioners to the Society which organized them into a board, advertised for public subscriptions and, usually within a year, a school had opened 'For the children of the labouring poor'.[16] The charity school curriculum comprised the three Rs with religious instruction and a few handicrafts intended to inure the children to an inevitable future of hard labour.

Somewhat surprisingly the movement's very achievements worried some for it appeared to challenge the absolute truth that the social station of everybody was fixed by God at birth. In 1732 Bernard Mandeville publicly attacked the prevailing 'Enthusiastick Passion' for charity schools arguing that 'the more a Shepherd, a Plowman or any other Peasant knows of the World, and the things that are Foreign to his Labour or Employment, the less fit he'll be to go through the Fatigues and Hardships of it with Chearfulness and Content'.[17] However Mandeville went further than most critics when he asserted that 'nothing should be taught for nothing but at Church . . . for if Parents are so miserably Poor that they can't afford their Children these first Elements of Learning, it is Impudence in them to aspire any further'.

Mandeville need not have worried. The charity school movement or 'Queen Anne's glory' as it was popularly known, did not last into the second half of the century when English schooling was moulded to fit the requirements of an industrial revolution which demanded a working childhood. In its early years the movement had gained dissenter and sometimes Roman Catholic allegiances but, in time, it turned High Church in character; while the organizing energy of the SPCK was diverted to overseas mission fields and the under-writing of a massive religious publishing business. By the late eighteenth century, English schooling for the lower classes, for all its minorities of Edgeworths busily inventing child-centred curricula or Sarah Trimmers introducing spinning into schools (on weekdays), had become enslaved to industrial capitalism which propounded an economic nationalism. Industry absorbed a cheap, seemingly inexhaustible supply of child labour in its search for optimum profits. In the circumstances the Sunday school movement became the ersatz mass education catering for the working child by teaching him to read on his one day off.

In so far as they served the lower classes, both the dame schools and the charity school movement had a special appropriateness and usefulness for New South Wales where the children were predom-inantly the offspring of poorly-paid marines' or convicts' wives. Yet there were limitations to the practicability of transplanting these English institutions for there was no 'middling class' or endowed church in the colony to maintain charity schools and many colonial parents were too poor to pay even the miserable fees necessary to keep a dame school teacher in business. It was evident that should schools of this kind open, they would require support from the government or from some other powerful sponsor if they were to survive for long.

While men do not act with a sketch-map of historians' reasons in their heads, a situation favourable to local initiation in education and an idea of the kind of schools required were the prerequisites for the opening of the first colonial schools. Nevertheless the diversion to educational purposes of the colony's scanty resources had always to be weighed against the demands of a community where survival itself was in the balance. Hence when schools did open and staff were selected to teach in them, the governor did not release his most able for teachers or spare the labour to accommodate the classes in well-constructed buildings designed exclusively as schools.

Chapter III

PRECEDENTS IN PUBLIC EDUCATION

Better build schoolrooms for 'the boy'
Than cells and gibbets for 'the man'.

ELIZA COOK
A Song for the Ragged Schools

Education in New South Wales began informally with the few artisans among the convicts and seamen passing on their crafts to the unskilled convicts and boys who were set to manufacturing bricks, stripping timber and plastering and thatching. No school-teacher appointed by the British government accompanied the Fleet although in the holds of the transports *Alexander* and the *Lady Penrhyn* were the convicts William Richardson and Isabella Rosson who were both teaching in the colony early in the 1790s. Phillip had reason to expect that schoolmasters would be sent out from England but his hopes failed to materialize.[1] The probable reason was that the funds of the SPG, the group most likely to have sponsored them, had been depleted by the heavy commitments its directors had made to the cause of the American Loyalists in Canada.[2] When approached for aid for the colony, they could afford only a few subsidies of £10 per annum and Phillip was told to find his teachers locally. It was obvious to the directors at home that schoolmasters could not readily be recruited to work in a penal settlement unless an attractive salary was guaranteed, for trained men easily earned £60 a year in England and an additional £20 to £40 above this sum or other inducements would have been required to entice them to New South Wales.[3]

The first schoolteacher in New South Wales was Isabella Rosson, *ex* the transport *Lady Penrhyn*, who apparently started a class on her own account sometime in 1789. The evidence supporting her claim rests on a statement by her husband, William Richardson, at the Select Committee on Transportation of 1812 in which he asserted that Isabella was a schoolmistress when he married her on 5 September 1789.

Was you married at Botany Bay?—Yes.

Did you marry one of the convicts?—Yes.

Had she a pardon upon her marriage?—No, she had served her time out before we were married.

In what situation was she?—She was a schoolmistress.[4]

This evidence from Richardson was corroborated in part by the statement by Johnson that 'a Person of the name of Richardson, together with his wife, began to teach a few Children at Sydney about the beginning of the year Ninety'.[5]

The thirty-three-year-old Isabella Rosson described herself as a mantua worker when she was tried at the Central Criminal Court Sessions on 10 January 1787 on the charge of

> . . . feloniously stealing, on the 5th of September last, one tambour muslin waistcoat, value 2s. the property of Stewart Kydd, Gent.
>
> A second count. For feloniously stealing, on the 13th of November last, four bed curtains, value 6s. his property.
>
> A third count. For feloniously stealing, on the 12th of December, one set of cotton bed curtains, value 4s. her property.[6]

On Kydd's evidence, Isabella, who was working for him as a laundress at the time, had always 'behaved exceedingly well to all appearance' and was given access to the cellar in his Gray's Inn chambers where she had stolen the materials from a trunk. When charged with the theft, Isabella 'fell down on her knees, and begged for mercy'. Kydd told her that she had 'behaved ungrateful' but was of a mind 'to forgive her, because she pleaded distress; I enquired into the distress, and the enquiry did not turn out in her favour'. The distress was that Isabella was pregnant at the time—her infant son John was to die a few days out from Plymouth.

Mrs Kydd was the next witness called. She told how she had gone down to the cellar

> . . . and the prisoner seeing me advance up to the trunks to open them, she immediately fell on her knees, and cried out, Madam, I have robbed you; says I, I know very well, Bella you have robbed me all along; you have been a very great deception; says she, Madam, I have robbed you of more than you know of; you need not open the trunks, for I have taken out all the bed curtains; I said, what could tempt you? she said Madam, do what you please with me, kill me, I deserve it, if I had twenty lives; says I, you deserve no mercy from me.

Isabella was brought before a justice where she confessed to having pawned the articles. After the pawnbroker's evidence was taken, she addressed the judge and jury in a single sentence, 'I leave myself to the mercy of the Court'. The Middlesex jury found her guilty and she was sentenced to be transported for seven years.

When Johnson spoke of Richardson at Sydney, the surname of a second schoolmistress named Johnson was also mentioned.[7] It appears likely that she was Mary Johnson who arrived aboard the *Mary Ann* in July 1791.[8] A servant girl like Isabella, Mary had been convicted of having stolen and pawned 'a cotton gown, value 6d. a yard of printed linen, value 2s.6d. a flat iron, value 4d. one linen clout, value 6d.'[9] It must be noted that such court charges do not always represent the real value of the goods stolen for British juries were sometimes reluctant to come out for the prosecution if the amount of a property theft made it mandatory for the judge to pass the death sentence. In some instances prisoners were deliberately arraigned on lesser charges in order to increase the Crown's chances of conviction. Keeping this in mind, the fact remains that the colony's first schoolmistresses were recruited from a pair of petty thieves convicted of stealing goods worth 12s. and 3s.10d. respectively.

The conviction of Isabella's schoolmaster husband, William Richardson, is described in the records of the Central Criminal Court of 1783, case no. 8.

> William Maynard and William Richardson were indicted for feloniously assaulting George Noble, on the King's highway, on the 1st of November last, and putting him in fear and danger of his life, and feloniously taking from his person and against his will, one handkerchief, value 1s. one guinea, value 21s. one crown piece, value 5s. a silver sixpence, and six copper halfpence, his property.
> Guilty. Death. They were both humbly recommended to mercy by the Jury.[10]

At the end of the sessions beginning 25 February 1784, the sentence was remitted on condition of transportation for seven years. Originally destined for transportation to Africa, Richardson was held aboard a hulk until the Fleet sailed and by the time it reached Botany Bay he had already served more than half his sentence.

Richardson was luckier than most convicts, he was not put to hard public labour but instead was assigned as servant to Captain Meredith of the Marines. He worked for Meredith until his time was out and, when the captain returned to England, Richardson joined the New South Wales Corps as a private at a guinea a month.[11] Despite the claims of a military career, Richardson still found time for his school and he appeared on Johnson's gratuity list for schoolmasters from 1793 on. Isabella and William Richardson returned to England with their children in 1810 where they kept up a correspondence with their friend and benefactor, Johnson, for whom

Richardson had acted part-time as parish clerk.[12] Two years later Richardson was chosen to give evidence at the Select Committee on Transportation on the state of the colony where he stood before his superiors as a reminder of one of the happier outcomes of their penal experiment.

The situation which saw convicts and ex-convicts employed as schoolteachers, when in the opinion of many the future depended on the proper upbringing of the children, may be partly explained by the dictates of necessity for no obvious alternative labour pool existed. It also reflected the diminished level of prejudice towards the employment of convicts in a penal colony where a man's measure came to be assessed on his day-to-day performances rather than by the category of his particular crime. Lastly, it was testimony to the colonists' remarkable faith in the efficacy of the education process itself. Precedents for using convicts as schoolmasters came from the era of American transportation. George Washington's father had purchased a bondsman to teach his son and the man had also served as sexton, church-cleaner and grave-digger. Again in Britain in 1794 Wilberforce had recommended to the government that 'proper people'[13] be selected from among the better disposed of the convicts to teach in colonial public schools.

The employment of women as teachers had much to do with the governor's difficulty in keeping that sex gainfully employed. Apart from the intermittent chores of minding children, some seasonal work in the fields, the running up of the scant supplies of cloth and occasionally collecting shells to burn for lime, many convict women found little to do of which a governor would have approved. A characteristic attitude of officialdom was put by the deputy judge advocate on the arrival of the Second Fleet. Collins thought it 'not a little mortifying to find on board the first ship that arrived, a cargo so unnecessary and unprofitable as two hundred and twenty-two females'.[14] With physical labour at a premium, it was unlikely that Phillip would have sanctioned the release of able-bodied men for teaching if suitable women were available especially as the classes contained mostly very young children. By the end of the 1790s though, when the uncertainties of the early years had passed and the child population had become representative of the various age groups, men were commonly preferred as elementary teachers except where classes were exclusively for infants or for girls.

For some convicts, selection as a teacher would have been a blessed relief from the wearisome drudgery of their day. Those convict women who were not selected for consorts or hut-keepers were 'set to make shirts, frocks, trowsers, etc. for the men, at a certain number per day; occasionally to pick grass in the fields, and for a

very slight offence are kept constantly at work the same as the men'.[15]
The lot of the typical male convict was far worse 'the discipline was
severe; the work unaccustomed, hard and constant; the punishments brutal and summary; the overseers harsh in the extreme'.
Yet teaching duties were not favoured solely because they were less
arduous physically than convict taskwork. They were also a good
route for the remission of sentences. Between September 1800, and
August 1806, King granted six men conditional or absolute pardons
for undertaking teaching duties.[16] Objections by local officials to the
employment of convicts or ex-convicts as schoolmasters are not in
evidence before the governorship of Lt General R. Darling in 1825.

The switch of employment from lace-maker to schoolteacher by
Isabella Rosson would have scarcely merited comment in the
eighteenth century when elementary teachers learned their skills on
the job. Further, Isabella's description of herself as a mantua worker
at her trial does not preclude the possibility that she had taught
classes in England before. The occupational status of her trade
ranked as high as that of dame schoolteacher and she may have
chosen to describe herself in what she considered would be her most
respected role. Even on the continent, where schoolmastering in
Protestant townships had more prestige as an occupation than was
the case in Britain, training was not a prerequisite for the post of
headmaster. One of the best known teachers in Europe and confidant
of Pestalozzi, Hermann Krüsi, had so far forgotten how to write for
a teaching post that he had to obtain a specimen of letters from a
writing master and had copied them hundreds of times over. He
obtained the headship of the local school regardless.[17] A similar
situation existed in New South Wales where the criteria for a schoolteacher did not extend much beyond literacy, good behaviour and
the ability to discipline a class.

Two years after Johnson had instituted his classes at Sydney and
Parramatta, he made the thousand nautical-mile trip in the *Sirius* to
to the sister settlement of Norfolk Island. Founded in 1788 under
Commandant P. G. King, Norfolk's population had been bolstered
two years later by a party of about 200 convicts shipped there in a
desperate attempt to preserve the dwindling food stocks on the mainland. The visit from the chaplain was timely for in his absence the
surgeon had performed the usual formalities of his office. In a short
hectic period of three days, Johnson married over a hundred couples,
baptized thirty-one children and noted that of eighty-five children
running footloose about thirty were of school age.[18]

Towards the end of 1793 King appointed 'a careful woman'[19] to
take charge of a small class and in 1794 Johnson discovered an
experienced teacher among the convicts. He was Thomas McQueen

who had taught school near Holborn, London, before receiving the sentence of seven years transportation in January 1790, for stealing

> . . . one feather-bed, value 2 L. two sheets, value 6s. two flat irons, value 1s. a copper tea-kettle, value 18d. a tea board, value 9d. a looking glass, value 2s. a glass salt holder, value 1d. a milk pot, value 3d. a bed quilt, value 2s. a brass candlestick, value 3d. a feather bolster, value 1s. the property of John Adams, in a lodging room . . . Articles were pawned.[20]

The man soon found himself teaching again in an old hut under the supervision of the chaplain of the New South Wales Corps, the Rev. J. Bain, 'a peevish old Battchellor'.[21]

King built a stone schoolhouse (56' x 18' x 9') for McQueen in 1794. It took twenty men three months to complete at a cost of £204 and the British treasury met the bill.[22] The commandant then appointed Susannah Hunt, a convict woman in her forties, who had been sentenced to seven years transportation but who was otherwise regarded as 'well qualified for her situation'.[23] She was set to teaching 'the young children'. King went on to open a small orphanage for about a dozen children and engaged William Mitchell, a seaman-turned-settler, to manage it.[24] By August 1795, this educational enthusiast, whom Marsden described as a man whose whole attention seemed occupied 'in promoting the real interest of those he has the honour to command',[25] had made provision for the education of seventy-five of the island's children. One schoolhouse was in the township of Sydney and the second close to the flag staff on nearby Mount George.[26]

Unfortunately for King, he was never able to recruit suitable staff. In 1799 McQueen was reported for drunkenness, then jailed for debt,[27] although he returned to teaching afterwards, while Mitchell's wife was described by the acting-commandant as having behaved 'as Ill if not worse, but such is our Situation were I to dismiss her, I do not know any one that could supply her Place'.[28] For a short time some of the Norfolk Island children were taught by the Rev. J. Harris, a missionary who had served as acting chaplain after Bain returned home, but his school was too far out of the township to be convenient for most day pupils.[29]

With over 750 convicts to choose from, acceptable teachers could be obtained more readily than the skilled labour and materials required for building schools. This was in spite of the fact that the building methods and materials used in the colony were of the most primitive kind. Ships' boats collected the cabbage tree for the wall-fillings of the huts, upright and cross-number posts were cut from local timber, and the walls were plastered over with clay before the roofs were thatched. A chimney was built of stones and spaces were left for windows which were sometimes latticed with twigs. The result by colonial standards was 'a very good hovel'.[30] Even when locally fired bricks became available, the buildings still lacked permanence because of a shortage of lime. Lime for mortar could only be produced in limited quantities by the arduous process of burning shells and coral or at the expense of shipping it from England. In its absence, the bricks were bound together by a stiff clay which rapidly deteriorated in the humidity of the east coast climate.

Buildings specifically designed as schools or church schools had no place in a community whose priorities were a hospital, storehouses, barracks, a wharf, and the thatching of tents and huts. So far as schools were concerned, the best indicator of their chances was that a permanent church did not open for worship at Parramatta until 1803[31] while Sydney still went without. In the circumstances, day schools in their own right were just not considered. The lone structure testifying to the colonists' concern with theoretical knowledge was an observatory built in 1788 to house the instruments sent out by the Board of Longitude for the observation of a comet.[32] No record remains of where Isabella's class of 1789 was accommodated but most likely it was held in a tent or in one of the smaller huts housing the families of convicts put up before the first winter.

Tired of waiting for a church which would also serve for a day school to work its way to the top of the essential buildings list, Johnson made the decision in 1793 to finance a construction of his own. Built of wattle and daub with a thatched roof, the church-school was cruciform in shape having a frontage 73' x 15' and transepts of 40' x 15'.[33] When completed it seated 500 with room for another 100 standing and had cost Johnson £67.12s. 11½d. of which he paid £59.18s. in dollars and cash and the rest in provisions including 20½ gallons of spirits.[34] Rum was a common means of payment in the colony; it was often difficult to get private or government work completed without resort to it. Governor Lachlan Macquarie's action in paying the annual rent of his colonial secretary's office in 80 gallons of rum was characteristic of the era.[35]

To assist Johnson in the erection of his 'temporary thatched house',[36] Acting-Governor Major Francis Grose grudgingly assigned two convicts to the job and supplied some materials from government supplies. But when the chaplain made an official claim for re-imbursement of his out-of-pocket expenses, Grose advised Secretary of State Dundas that he thought the cost excessive.[37] This brought the intercession of Wilberforce who pleaded that Johnson, 'one of the worthiest men breathing',[38] fully deserved repayment. Nevertheless the chaplain's request was turned down. Johnson then wrote to Dundas asking for his money back; and in the same letter in which he apologized to the secretary of state for causing 'differences', he managed to work in a complaint about his 'severe and oppressive treatment'.[39] The Rev. J. Newton, always the chaplain's sounding-board in England, counselled him to be patient[40] and Johnson was to recoup his outlay in Hunter's governorship after a two-year wait.

Johnson employed William Richardson, Isaac Nelson and Thomas Taber in the day school which opened in the church building. Nelson had been sentenced to seven years transportation in 1789; and Taber, a watch-finisher by trade, was sentenced to life imprisonment in 1796.[41] The three men were working in separate schools in Sydney when Johnson returned from Norfolk Island but following the construction of the temporary church, the chaplain obtained Hunter's permission to consolidate the schools under the one roof 'thus to unite in their Endeavours for the better Improvement of their scholars'.[42] However at seven o'clock on the evening of 1 October 1798, smoke was noticed coming from the building's thatched roof. Tinder-dry and of combustible material the church was gutted in an hour.[43] As it stood alone and was deserted after school hours, the building was probably fired deliberately, most likely in retaliation for Hunter's enforcement of the rule which required the attendance of convicts at divine service regardless of their personal religious beliefs. The governor offered a £30 reward and a free pardon to an informant[44] but without result. The school was removed to the court house and, when parents complained at the irregular hours caused by the frequency of the court hearings, it was moved again to a disused storehouse. The immediate result of holding school in the cold and damp store was that enrolments halved.[45]

Problems in school accommodation were not to be overcome in Johnson's chaplaincy. Not withstanding the disabilities of housing, the teachers selected by the chaplain secured and maintained for a period an astonishingly high level of school enrolments. A government school with continuity of operation had opened at Sydney early in 1792 for a child population of about ninety and another at Parramatta for forty odd.[46] In 1794 there was a class for approximately sixty-five children at Norfolk Island[47] where two schools and an orphanage were serving a child population of around 200[48] two years later.

The situation in New South Wales contrasted with early nineteenth-century England where the demand for child labour saw seven-year-olds recruited for the coalmines and where masters would apprentice paupers to the manufacturers in a deal which included an idiot child with every nineteen sane. In the most recently industrialized English counties, the numbers attending school fell to below five in a hundred.[49] In 1816 a Select Committee working on the assumption that one-ninth of the population was between seven and thirteen, estimated that one child in sixteen was enrolled in England and one in twenty in Wales.[50] However, at Sydney in 1798, Johnson's convict-taught day school had an enrolment of at least 150[51] and this figure does not include those who attended the military school. Yet the entire child population of the township was barely 400 boys and girls,[52] many of whom had not yet reached their third birthdays when they were considered old enough to attend school regularly.

Chapter IV

GOVERNMENT TEACHERS AND
PUBLIC SCHOOLS:
THE SECOND PHASE

> ... I wish you would send out a few persons
> with small salaries to take on them the office
> of schoolmasters; I say small salaries,
> because if you were to give large ones
> improper people would accept the situa-
> tions; if you would let me look out for a few
> persons fit for the purpose I should be greatly
> obliged to you; and I trust you know me
> well enough to believe me, with't reserva-
> tions, that I make the proposal, not because
> I have four or five people that I wish to do
> jobs for, but because I am desirous of pro-
> moting the temporal and eternal happiness
> of the people who are in question.
>
> W. WILBERFORCE to H. DUNDAS[1]

By the early 1800s, the terms public schoolmaster and public school
were a part of everyday usage in the colony. However they were
applied in a sense quite different from their meaning in England
where a public school typically described an endowed institution
which enrolled fee-paying boarders exclusively and whose headmaster was in holy orders. By comparison the colonial public school
was a day school for the children of the lower classes, many of whom
could not afford to pay fees; and a public schoolmaster was a convict
or ex-convict kept by the government. Although the colonial
teacher had not yet attained the recognition which went with a
regular Crown salary, the designation *public* placed him in the lowest
strata of petty officialdom along with the public shoemaker, the
public tailor, the public clerk and the public butcher.[2]

A break in the precedent of employing convict and ex-convict
teachers came when William Webster, a private in the New South
Wales Corps, and his free-born wife Margaret opened a school at
the order of the Corp's commander, Major Francis Grose in 1792.

The New South Wales Corps had been raised in 1789 by Grose who had contracted to recruit the 300 men required for the Botany Bay outpost himself provided he could sell the unit's captaincies and lieutenancies at the market price and pocket the difference between the three guineas subsidy from the Crown and the actual sum each recruit cost him to sign on.[3] The takers at Grose's prices were drawn from among the unskilled and the unemployed and were well below normal standards for the British Army, this at a time when the red coat was admitted to be 'a badge less of honour, than of shame'.[4]

Webster had joined the army as a twenty one-year-old in 1778[5] and had been ordered to teaching duties before the Corps embarked at Chatham along with three other privates whom Grose had 'pitched upon at present as the most proper for executing the office of schoolmasters'.[6] But Webster alone appears to have carried out the original plan after the advance party marched ashore at Port Jackson in February 1792. Certainly there were plenty of opportunities for Webster to practise his teaching skills for, apart from the children of the soldiers' wives, many of Grose's men were themselves illiterate. Some had been recruited from the military prisoners in the Savoy[7] and, in New South Wales, convicts were inducted into the ranks. It has been estimated that a quarter of the troops of the Corps in 1807 was composed of the criminal element of the British population and that many of the balance were little better.[8]

Grose's action in appointing military schoolmasters was noteworthy in that there was no continuous tradition of the employment of schoolmasters in the British army. Records of army schools overseas go back to 1662 when the officers of Fort St George, Madras, had employed a schoolmaster;[9] and the garrison at Tangiers possessed three in 1685, 'a graduate', 'a clerk and schoolmaster' and an 'usher, writing master, and gunner'.[10] The first record of army schools in England is dated 1762 when a class was kept by the First Regiment of the Guards at the Tower; and a set of model standing orders has survived from 1768 which recommended that

A Sergeant or Corporal, whose sobriety, honesty and good conduct can be depended upon, and who is capable of teaching Writing, Reading and Arithmetic, is to be employed in the capacity of a Schoolmaster, by whom *soldiers and soldiers' children* are to be carefully instructed.[11]

Instruction in the army was usually at the officers' expense being designed to eradicate adult illiteracy and to discipline the children of the numerous camp followers. The number of army schools increased towards the end of the eighteenth century until the adjutant-general instructed all commanding officers to establish regimental schools in 1811. Before then a decision as to whether or not a school would open was at the discretion of the individual com-mander. Grose's foresight in looking after the welfare of his men was also demonstrated by his engagement of Chaplain Bain. This was at a time when such appointments were commonly bestowed upon the parish clergy who had no obligation to follow the colours, a practice which had reduced the Duke of Wellington to one chaplain for his entire army.

Before the Corps left England, Grose had Bain submit the four schoolmasters' names to the directors of the SPG in the hope of committing the Society to finding their salaries and supplying text-books for their classes. Before Bain made formal application though, Grose briefed him to ensure that the Society understood that, unless Phillip thought otherwise, the teachers would be under military not civil control.[12] Grose wanted any money the Society granted lodged with his English agents preferably a year in advance 'as it must be a long time 'ere the money can be drawn'.[13] Meeting in January 1790, the Society's directors agreed in principle to Bain's request and they promised an allowance of £10 per annum for any four teachers the Major cared to nominate.[14]

When the directors came actually to pay their commitment they either forgot or else rejected Grose's precise conditions. Instead they channelled their money through Johnson who was in a quandary as to whether he should pay it exclusively to the teachers of the Corps, or whether part of it could be legitimately expended on the chaplain's civil teachers.[15] The point took time to resolve. Phillip's permission was also necessary before the money could be accepted and payment was delayed further by the fact that Bain had kept the Society's original promise in his pocket from September 1791 until March 1792.[16] Not until 1795 were the directors in a position to confirm their commitment of 1790 which they extended to cover Johnson's nominees.[17]

Richardson on Johnson's certification and Webster on Bain's, received the first of the Society's grants of £10 for teaching in 1793-4.[18] With the money they could have purchased 20 bushels of wheat or 25 lbs or fresh pork or 10 gallons of Jamaica rum; or else they could have hired an unskilled labourer for four months or have had eight acres of their land cleared at the fixed government rate. This £10 proved Webster's last for he was struck off Johnson's list for 'having turned out an infamous character'.[19] Richardson kept himself in the chaplain's good graces longer. By 1798 he had received his second £10 gratuity for services up to 1794-5, and, the year following, Nelson and Taber shared Webster's disputed allowance between them.[20] In 1799 Richardson was paid another £30 for teaching up to 1798.[21]

These delays indicated what an attenuated business the payment procedure was, for the English directors would not pass a bill unless they had approved each individual's name in advance. In the ten years that it took for them to accept the names of Richardson, Webster, McQueen and Hunt only £20 was actually paid into the chests of Johnson's agent, Ambrose Martin, Esq., of Finch Lane, Cornhill. Meeting in July, 1800,[22] the directors agreed to pay Johnson the £50 balance they owed him which the chaplain had already advanced to his teachers, but the Norfolk Islanders had to wait on King's certification in 1801 before they became eligible for their money. Cash gratuities from the Church of England augmented the income of several colonial teachers up to 1830 however its significance in the total pattern of school aid was more by way of a lucky windfall for the recipient than a reliable source of funds for colonial education.

In their efforts to keep convict and emancipist schoolmasters teaching, the governors resorted to various means of remuneration short of paying them an official salary. In 1792 Phillip promised Johnson that he would guarantee a living from teaching to all schoolmasters prepared to come out. However he did not expect them to be a heavy charge on the public.[23] In a letter soliciting teachers from Dundas, Wilberforce had put the matter in its contemporary perspective when he suggested 'small salaries, because if you were to give large ones improper people would accept the situations'.[24] Phillip proved more generous. He offered teachers land grants and convict servants in an attempt to induce them to the colony and meantime agreed that any ex-convicts selected for teaching should remain on the stores. He also decided to distribute the Society's grants through official government channels thereby saving the otherwise inevitable small bills for discount services.[25]

Where a schoolmaster's income was cash or a money gratuity, payment was most often in 'currency', the name given to the private promissory notes and revalued copper coin which comprised the colony's internal money made necessary by the shortage of specie. Because their soldiers' pay came in currency, Webster and Richardson were effectively prevented from purchasing from vessels in the harbour as their captains would not accept this local money. Consequently teachers were forced to purchase through the colony's notoriously rapacious middle-men. Not until Bligh reformed military pay procedures by issuing negotiable bills were these teachers able to purchase the goods they needed directly from visiting merchant captains.

Although schoolmasters who taught the children of the poor without charge received a government ration for their trouble, this required supplementation if a man was to improve his standard of living. When ex-convicts became eligible for land grants, the opportunity opened for them to become part-time farmers. Among the first recipients of land were Richardson who was granted 75 acres in the district of the Eastern Farms and Webster who received 30 acres at York Place.[26] Both Nelson and Taber raised sufficient meat on their grants to sell the surplus to the government stores. The opportunity to work and own land, the number of a teacher's children being reckoned in the size of the grant, was additional to a teacher's other sources of income which typically included a Society gratuity, rations and the occasional assigned convict, as well as the right to hold down a second job like that of coroner, parish clerk or private in the Corps, and to collect what fees he could in cash or kind.

In the schools of Isabella Rosson and Mary Johnson, the schoolmistresses 'taught the Children belonging to *Convicts* gratis—the Military officers &c making them some little acknowledgement for their trouble'.[27] But by the time Richardson, Nelson and Taber were teaching in the temporary church more formal arrangements had become necessary. Parents were required to pay an enrolment fee of sixpence per child and, for each 'as are learning to read, to pay four pence pr week—those learning to write, or arithmetic, six pence'.[28] The fees were high. A family of four taking the full curriculum would have cost their parents 26s. for their first quarter at school, a sum equivalent to the monthly wage of a kept servant at the fixed government rates. However, Johnson's rules contained the proviso that children from poor families would not be charged, this decision being left 'to the Judgement and Humanity of the Schoolmasters'.

Sometimes a master would use a public school appointment as a stepping stone to a more lucrative career. Nelson opened a private academy and his pupils were presented at Government House in January 1804, when King 'was pleased personally to examine into the progress of their Education, on which occasion Mrs. King also assisted'.[29] Afterwards 'His EXCELLENCY was pleased to confer a Donation upon the children, as an encouragement to future emulation, and to promise a further notice in proportion as their assiduity might hereafter recommend them'. In 1809 Nelson received a land grant from Lieutenant Governor William Paterson[30] and he opened his third school on a hundred-acre grant at Prospect Creek where he was teacher, stock-keeper and horticulturist.

Taber, who had received a full pardon for his teaching services by June 1806,[31] was equally as successful as Nelson. Giving up his public school, the tall, sharp-featured man with his lank straight hair who was rarely seen in his shirt sleeves in school time,[32] opened a small private academy in Sydney. There the respectable 'Vestry Clerk of the Parish of St. Philip' promised parents 'who may please to place their children under his tuition' that they could be assured of 'the strictest attention to their speedy improvement in Reading, Writing, Arithmetic, Book-keeping, etc. on the most reasonable terms'.[33] Taber too received a land grant from Paterson of 60 acres which he worked part-time to help support his free-born wife and their five children. The grant was treated with some concern for its future worth, the master passing his land down as a legacy for his heirs.

Special recognition of Taber's services came from Governor Sir T. Brisbane in 1824 after the schoolmaster had memorialized the governor for 'a small pension in recognition of his twenty-five years as a teacher of reading, writing and the duties of religion and morality'.[34] Just before he retired, Taber was managing quite well in the Second Sydney Public School on an income of £30 per annum in salary, a Society allowance of £10, school fees and an allowance as parish clerk paid from the Police Fund.[35] This was exclusive of whatever his farming activities were returning. The Church of England clergyman, Rev. W. Cowper, endorsed the memorial with the comment that Taber was a 'very moral and peaceable man, always diligent and attentive to his duty and most respectful in his behaviour'. To assist Brisbane in deciding an appropriate pension, Colonial Secretary Goulburn submitted a list of the government's other minor pensioners. They were J. Gowen who had given 23 years' service at 5s. a day and J. Tucker with 32 years' service at 3s. a day. Both had been granted a yearly pension of £50. Brisbane decided to pay Taber the same sum from 20 September 1824.

Of the many ingenious solutions devised to maintain colonial schools, the one which ultimately proved the most effective, was originally applied by King at Norfolk Island to help support destitute children.

> Except the Cloathing, the Stores afford no comforts or necessaries for Children of this Age, & still less for Infants; (Which last description are much indebted to a Private Charity of the Marchioness of Buckingham's). In order to provide those Children who are Grown up, with some necessaries, I directed all Fines, and Forfeitures, to be paid into the hands of the Chaplain for that use, Not more than six Pounds have been forfeited during the last two Years, which Fines have been for Breaches of the Peace, But small as the sum is, it has enabled the Children to make a very decent appearance.[36]

King turned to the same solution when his schools needed money but this time more methodically by directing that court fees, fines for illegal trading and port duties go into a separate school fund. Imposts for the school began in 1794 when the lieutenant-governor ordered that half of a 20s. fine, imposed on a settler for punching a soldier on the nose, be spent on the school.[37] At the close of that year, King formalized arrangements through a General Order:

Imports

On the arrival of Ships The Masters & others who have Merchandize to dispose of, are to declare what they have for sale, & the Price of each article—

No Articles to be bought or sold untill the Price is fixed—

No payment for Spirits or Wine, will be taken Cognizance of by a Magistrate where the price shall exceed,
For Spirits ... 5s/p^r Quart Wine Measure
For Wine .. 4/ Do ... Do —

Every Person Convicted before the Magistrates of selling by other, than just Weights & Measures, or who shall adulterate, or alter the Quality of any Articles which may be retailed, will for the First offence forfeit the Sum of Forty Shillings, for the Second Fifty Six Shillings; & for the Third Offence will forfeit Five Pounds & be put in the Pillory for Three Hours, All Forfeitures to be applied to the use of the School—

The following Regulation was also made, which I had Two Views in proposing, the first was to throw every obstacle in the way to prevent, Spirits being brought to the Island, & the Second was, to make such Quantity's as might be brought here, serviceable to the Children, among whom were many helpless Children deserted by their Parents; The object of which was to oblige the Master of a Ship or other 'Persons', Importing Spirits or Wine into this Island to pay into the Hands of the Chaplain for the use of the School for every Ten Gallons of Rum or other Spirits—
Four Shillings
Do ... Fifteen Gallons of Wine Cyder &c.[38]

King's act was illegal. However, cavils on legality did not prevent him from applying the identical principle when he took up his mainland governorship and his customs dues were continued and extended by his successors. Certainly small sums had been paid to the colonial administration for liquor permits and licences before but King had taken the logical next step by systematically raising a revenue. In 1818 a validating act had to be hurriedly rushed through the British Parliament to legitimize these payments and a second was needed five years later to make the act perpetual. Unfortunately the private sector of the island's economy was never buoyant enough to ensure the Norfolk Island schools much of an income beyond paying for a few schoolbooks and some items of clothing for the scholars.

When King replaced Hunter as governor in September 1800, the colony's public schools were accommodated in private houses or in government buildings loaned temporarily for the purpose. Yet for all the new governor's faith in the native born, who 'alone can be regarded as fixed to the soil',[39] he too baulked at the expense of building permanent schools for them promising instead a government subsidy towards school buildings if the local community was willing to raise the balance by subscription. On a tour of the Hawkesbury district in 1802 King counted over 200 children and he offered the settlers assistance in erecting a school and chapel provided they met a substantial part of the cost themselves.[40]

King deputed the Hawkesbury school as serving the scattered settlements of Richmond Hill, Phillip, Prospect Hill, Baulkam Hills, Northern Boundaries, Field of Mars and Eastern farms. However, the settlers did not warm to the governor's plan for their own good and in the two years which followed few subscriptions were collected. This left King no option other than to build the chapel-school himself. Before he commenced building though, the governor demanded that the settlers raise a land tax of 2d. an acre for fourteen years in return for a Crown lease of the building and ground. The money was to be applied to the support of a clergyman and a schoolmaster.[41] The residents voted in favour of King's plan and a paper agreeing to his conditions was signed by six landowners with holdings of at least 100 acres and by the magistrates W. Cox and Marsden.

The method of raising money by a levy on land was a common source of government revenue in England and schools had been supported in New England by income from land grants. But the New South Wales variant whereby the government built the school and then leased it to the local community was a typically colonial solution. There is no evidence that King collected any of his land tax. The impost was probably suspended after the severe Hawkesbury floods of 1806 and King attempted no similar ventures. He contented himself with maintaining teachers and left them to accommodate their classes where best they could.

When King left the colony in 1806, his government was employing three schoolmasters at Sydney (one taught a class of Roman Catholic children), two at Parramatta, and three at the settlements of Toongabbie, Kissing Point and Green Hills.[42] In his support of a Roman Catholic school, King displayed an uncommon degree of religious tolerance for, although the communion was about a quarter of the population, it was in a more depressed state in New South Wales than in Erastian England. Before the Fleet had sailed, two Irish priests petitioned Lord Sydney to be allowed to minister in the colony.[43] They were refused. So too were a group of local Catholics who memorialized the home government for a minister in 1792.[44] The first Catholic priests to come to New South Wales arrived as convicts: Fathers Dixon, O'Neil and Harold were transported for alleged complicity in the Irish Rebellion of 1798. Four years later Lord Hobart instructed King to grant the men conditional emancipations.[45] He also suggested that the governor employ them either as schoolmasters or in the exercise of their clerical functions.

Following Hobart's direction King permitted the 'exemplary'[46] Fr Dixon to celebrate Mass in 1803 and allowed him a government stipend of £60 per annum.[47] But while King trusted Dixon the man, he was watchful of a congregation which lived in such 'credulous ignorance that an artful priest may lead them to every action that is either good or bad'.[48] After the insurrection of Irish convicts at Castle-hill in 1804 King stopped Dixon celebrating Mass; this was irrespective of the fact that the priest had rode with the government soldiers.

Although King permitted a Roman Catholic layman to teach a class of children of his own persuasion, he remained adamantly opposed to the employment of priests as teachers. Such a concession, he alleged, would give them the 'means, were they so disposed, of instilling improper ideas into the minds of their pupils'.[49] The exception was Fr Harold who taught a public school at Norfolk Island where he lived 'a poor, honest, industrious, moral man'[50] until he left the island in 1809.

By the eighteenth century, Roman Catholic elementary schools had opened in England and there were a few academies for the wealthy. It was in one of these that Alexander Pope had been whipped for whiling away the hours by writing satires on his masters. The Roman Catholic population of London had increased after the French Revolution and its teachers gained some relief from 32 Geo. III C32 of 1792 whereby 'no Ecclesiastic or other Person professing the *Roman* Catholic religion, who shall take and subscribe the Oath of Allegiance, Abjuration, and Declaration . . . shall be prosecuted in any Court whatsoever, for teaching and instructing Youth as a Tutor or Schoolmaster, any Law or Statute to the contrary not withstanding'. Nevertheless a Roman Catholic schoolmaster had to have his name registered by the Clerk of the Peace at the Quarter Sessions, he was forbidden to receive into his school 'the Child of any Protestant Father', and he could not hold 'the Mastership of any College or School of Royal Foundation, or of any other endowed College or School for the Education of Youth, or shall keep a School in either of the Universities of *Oxford* and *Cambridge*'.

The act also forbade the founding of orders bound by religious or monastic vows.

The first official mention of a Roman Catholic school in New South Wales comes in King's dispatch of 12 August 1806.[51] Its teacher was probably Jeremy Cavanagh who had been granted a conditional pardon for his services as 'Catholic Schoolmaster'.[52] Another early Roman Catholic teacher was the ex-convict James Kenny, who kept a private school in the Rocks district of Sydney. In an advertisement in *The Sydney Gazette*, Kenny agreed to pay 'the strictest attention' to his pupils and their 'speedy improvement in Reading, Writing, Vulgar and Decimal Arithmetic, Mensuration, and Book-keeping according to the Italian mode'.[53] Kenny gave up his school at Sydney in Bligh's time and re-opened it at Wilberforce where the master had a small farm.[54] State-aided Roman Catholic schools with any degree of continuity did not appear until the end of Macquarie's governorship. Before that time, Marsden's boast to Wilberforce that 'Roman Catholics, Jews, and persons of all persuasions, send their children to the public schools where they are all instructed in the principles of our established religion'[55] was based on fact.

The existence of six government-sponsored mainland schools was an impressive achievement and King was well aware of this when he listed them in one of his last important dispatches, part of a futile attempt to salvage something of his reputation at home as a colonial administrator. Unhappily these educational gains, commendable though they were, proved inadequate measures of a governor's efficiency in Downing Street. By 1806 King's regime had drawn to its acrimonious close. His declared policies clashed with those of the powerful trading interests who deployed 'art, cunning, and fraud'[56] in pursuit of their private ends and King had failed to subdue them. Then there was the mud-raking of his Norfolk Island liaison with a convict woman which led to vicious public lampooning and to King's over-eager, often pathetic requests for an open enquiry into all aspects of his services to New South Wales.

Bligh (of the *Bounty* fame), who succeeded King as governor, was the first career man to take the post and the authorities had to double the salary to obtain his services. Bligh's name appears in the Admiralty records for 1762 when he was entered on the books of H.M.S. *Monmouth* at seven years of age as servant of Captain K. Stewart.[57] The entry was a nominal one designed to evade the essential qualification for a naval lieutenancy, that a candidate must have served six years at sea. In 1770 Bligh began his adventurous career when he was listed an able-bodied seaman on the pay sheets of H.M.S. *Hunter*. Yet Bligh's limited formal education does not appear to have restricted his range of intellectual interests. Before he took command of New South Wales, the governor elect attempted to put together a library for Government House. Among the books he selected were: Blackstone's *Commentaries*, a science encyclopedia, Linnaeus's system, Dr Johnson's *Dictionary*, Adam Smith's *Wealth of Nations*, Malthus on *Population* and Gibbon's *Decline and Fall of the Roman Empire*.[58]

Bligh's Instructions from the Crown contained the traditional stipulation of a 200-acre endowment for a public schoolmaster and, ironically in the light of King's efforts, he was directed to pay special attention to education.[59] The new governor moved energetically to obey orders. He visited all the Sydney schools, selected sites for schools on his tours of the outlying settlements and kept up the review of schoolchildren at Government House. Bligh also wrote to the Tory politician, Castlereagh, to recruit four teachers for the public schools and a married couple to manage the orphanage. The peer replied, in effect, that he was prepared to make the appointments if he could be given the names of men willing to come out.[60] But it was not until Marsden returned to England in 1807 and personally recruited three men that trained schoolmasters were obtained for the colonial service.

Developments in public education in New South Wales came to an abrupt end in 1808 when Bligh was deposed by a military junta in a rebellion which was the most spectacular enterprise of the New South Wales Corps since their mutiny aboard the female convict transport, *Lady Shore*, which they had sailed to Monte Video and personal oblivion. The coup was led by Captain J. Macarthur who, styling himself Colonial Secretary, took over the colony's civil affairs. Rev. H. Fulton, known to be loyal to Bligh, was replaced by W. P. Crook although the missionary was not trusted to preach during services, the naval officer was dismissed and the commissary arrested. Macarthur's military henchmen confiscated the public records, removed official ledgers and prepared victualling lists of their own.

The regime struck the Kissing Point public schoolmaster, Matthew Hughes, off the rations list, a victim apparently of an economy campaign designed to impress English critics. The master was forced to close his school for part of the week and labour in the fields to keep his family alive.[61] In fact stagnation in education was regression, for between 1807-10 the children on the mainland increased by nearly 1,000 to around 2,700, while the percentage attending school fell to its lowest point since 1791.[62] An effect of the rebellion was to draw the attention of the British authorities to instabilities in colonial society. The man they chose to re-impose Crown authority was Macquarie one of whose earliest decisions as governor was to launch a system of charity schools in every major settlement as part of his plans for facilitating social cohesion and re-asserting community discipline.

Chapter V

THEORY AND PRACTICE OF
A PUBLIC SCHOOL EDUCATION

Schools, or some system at least of regulated
education, in which industry and morals are
more attended to than is learning, should be
co-extensive with the youth of the settlement.

RT HON. SPENCER PERCEVAL
Chancellor of the Exchequer[1]

The school in the daub and wattle church in Hyde Park was
conceived in the Protestant vernacular tradition expounded by
Luther and Calvin in the sixteenth century. Calvin had insisted on
teaching in the vernacular in preference to Latin and his educational
theory stressed the usefulness of memorizing the catechism, psalm-
singing and the habit of worship. In the seventeenth century the
religious reformer's ideas spread to Scotland and Sweden where
Geneva-type systems were attempted and some Massachusetts townships made 'selectmen' responsible for teaching their young people
how to read the Bible in English, 'It being one chiefe project of yt
ould deluder, Sathan, to keepe men from the knowledge of ye
Scriptures'.[2]

Translations of the Bible into English had been instrumental in
breaking down the universality of Latin in Britain and educators like
Richard Mulcaster, head of Merchant Tailors, who accepted that
the mother tongue was the common heritage of all Britons, became
influential spokesmen for the doctrine that biblical literacy was an
Englishman's birthright. The Protestant clergy agreed. Although
they thought the catechism still the best path to salvation, they
believed that the way would be more brightly illumined if everyone
could read the Heavenly Father's Will for himself. They also argued
that the spread of vernacular translations would be a powerful antidote to the doctrinal trickeries of Roman works. Such was the
voracious appetite of Europeans for this kind of education that the
Roman Catholic Church joined the movement with De La Salle's
lay brothers instructing the children of the Paris poor in French in
1688.

44

The argument that teaching the masses to read was essential if Biblical truths were to be revealed to all was central to the religious beliefs of the English philanthropists of the 1790s who sponsored lending libraries, savings banks and Sunday schools. Their text, the Bible, was the world's cheapest book and they thought it equally good for man and child. Radical Wesleyan preachers whose leader exhorted them to spend at least five hours a day reading could thus unite in good conscience with the more orthodox Church of England followers of *Practical Christianity*. The educational programmes of both affirmed that if reading skills were applied to Bible, prayerbook and catechism, then, in| some apocalyptic way, the good life was assured.

The three basic concerns for pupils in attendance at Johnson's school were the catechism, reading, and regular attendance at divine service. Catechetical instruction was likened to 'a little watering pot to shed good lessons'[3] and prudent mothers were counselled to drop continually something of it on their children 'as Honey from the Rock'. There was considerable teaching content in *The Shorter Westminster Catechism* with its 107 questions and answers although a number of briefer catechisms had begun to appear in bookshops especially written for children three years of age and upwards. These contained such statements as '"What must become of you if you are wicked?" The answer to the last is, "If I am wicked, I shall be sent down to everlasting Fire in Hell among wicked and miserable creatures".'[4] The Hyde Park school children were required to memorize the church catechism and to recite it back to Johnson on Sundays.[5]

Johnson was following English precedent when he demanded that all his pupils attend church regularly. He required the attendance of the ex-convict teachers too, ostensibly for the purpose of noting absences but more probably to keep the child congregation in order. By enforcing the attendance of school children the chaplain may have hoped to attract their parents also, for colonists were reluctant churchgoers. And this could well have been one motive behind his suggestion that parents who so wished could remain behind after the service to hear their children say their lessons. This habit of 'a constant attendance on Divine Worship'[6] was urged on all parents as the only certain means of ensuring their children's 'future life secured by every good quality from the vicissitudes which are ever certain to result from bad examples and abandoned courses'. If a mother neglected to send her child to church then Johnson had the governor's authority to expel him.

At a quarter to nine each morning, Sundays excepted, the bell tolled to alert the children to set out for school. A few would find seats close to the windows while the rest perched themselves on the roughly-hewn pews in the semi-gloom, their legs dangling above the floor. Following contemporary practices the chief master would have viewed the assembly from the elevated preacher's rostrum as he watched his two colleagues usher their classes to the corners of the building as far apart as possible. Next to each man would be boxes for his canes and for the textbooks, paper, quills, slates, ink-powder and soft lead pencils. As yet there were no blackboards or steel nibs, and writing masters spent much of their time mending quills and demonstrating how to keep points on them.

The school supplies had been requisitioned by Johnson from the government stores. The commissariat held stocks of slates purchased at 4d. each, lead pencils at 3d., quills at 1s. for twenty[7] and ink-powder at 3d. a packet. Paper though was a scarce and expensive item at £1 a ream for foolscap of only average quality and little would have found its way into the classroom. Over the years there were periodic shortages of all items. Then the alphabet was scratched out on framed squares of moistened sand or by pipe-clay on tiles and the children dipped their magpie quills into home-made ink for writing on paper trimmings and scraps.[8]

The work day began with a prayer followed by a hymn. Evangelical clergy typically encouraged the singing of hymns for the practice was thought especially efficacious in inculcating religious truths and for conserving those of the heart. Johnson's hymns were chosen from the collection of Rev. Dr Isaac Watts, the celebrated dissenter and author of school textbooks in most areas of human knowledge. At the Latin school, Southampton, Watts had been taught Latin, Greek, Hebrew and French, and the youth continued his studies in divinity, ethics, geography, history, language, logic, mathematics, metaphysics, natural science, philosophy and rhetoric at Rowe's Academy in London.[9] Among his best-known works were *Divine and Moral Songs for the Use of Children*, and *Hymns and Spiritual Songs*, which went through sixteen editions between 1707 and 1748. Occasionally Watts succeeded in suppressing his Puritan conscience, which forbade an over-reliance on the imagination, for long enough to compose a number of charming verses for children of which 'Against Quarrelling and Fighting' is an outstanding example.

1.
Let Dogs delight to bark and bite,
For GOD has made them so;
Let bears and lions growl and fight,
For 'tis their nature too.

2.

But, children, you should never let
Such angry passions rise;
Your little hands were never made
To tear each other's Eyes.

3.

Let love through all your actions run,
And all your words be mild;
Live like the blessed Virgin's Son,
That sweet and lovely Child.

4.

His Soul was gentle as a Lamb;
And, as His stature grew,
He grew in favour both with man,
And GOD His Father too.

5.

Now, LORD of all, He reigns above,
And from His heav'nly throne
He sees what children dwell in love,
And marks them for His own.[10]

Schoolteachers generally approved Watts's sentiments and commented on them in their lessons. Mrs Cockle queried her readers: '"Why, it might be asked, did dogs delight, by nature, to bark and bite, if God had made all things good?" "Because" she explained "their nature had been changed by the sin of man".'[11] Another reason Watts was able to capture a healthy share of the British text-book market was his ability to write from a comparatively non-doctrinal Protestant position. In the preface of his children's song book he assured readers that they would find nothing within which

> . . . savours of a party: the children of high and low degree, of the Church of England or Dissenters, baptized in infancy or not, may all join together in these songs. And as I have endeavoured to sink the language to the level of a child's understanding, and yet to keep it, if possible, above contempt, so I have designed to profit all, if possible, and offend none.[12]

The doctor's claim that his work was inoffensive was not entirely correct for he was author of the notorious stanza:

LORD, I ascribe it to Thy grace,
And not to chance, as others do,
That I was born of Christian race,
And not a Heathen or a Jew.[13]

Some of Watts's other verse, though not objectionable in this sense, was obviously written with the purchaser in mind not the child.

AGAINST EVIL COMPANY

Why should I join with those in play
In whom I've no delight;
Who curse and swear, but never pray;
Who call ill names, and fight?

I hate to hear a wanton song,
Their words offend mine ears;
I should not dare defile my tongue
With language such as theirs . . .

My GOD, I hate to walk or dwell
With sinful children here:
Then let me not be sent to hell,
Where none but sinners are.[14]

When the opening prayer and hymn were concluded, the Hyde
Park school children lined up for the opportunity to read to their
masters. Early in the nineteenth century they were divided into
grades: the abc class; the 2, 3, 4, 5 letters class; the two syllables
class; and the Bible class.[15] These classes were divided again into
those writing with slate pencils and those using quills and paper. As
a child earned his place in a particular grade solely on his ability to
read, bearded illiterates could often be found learning alongside
infants in the abc class. Once they had mastered the alphabet, the
children practised building up letters into units ba, be, bi, bo, bu,
etc.; and, over the years, a few might reach the standard of an
advanced scholar who could spell out a - bo - mi - na - ti - on without
a stumble. The abc method of teaching reading was based on the
logical assumption that a letter was easier to learn than a syllable,
and that a syllable was easier to remember than a word or a
sentence.

The practice whereby a master heard each child in the queue
recite, then tested his memory and assigned the next task, was known
as 'the individual'. Apart from keeping order in the line, some masters undertook no other purposive teaching activities. What a child
learned was very much a matter for himself, or it depended on help
at home, or was the outcome of sitting beside a brighter pupil. Much
of the child's schoolday was spent in this unprofitable business of
learning nonsense syllables by heart and in unsteadily deciphering
short words. One observer likened reading aloud in colonial schools
to 'a *musical* performance consisting of a thousand repetitions of a
single note'.[16] This, he alleged, was the outcome of rote learning
and the ill-advised practice of teaching younger and older pupils in
the one class.

It sometimes happens, that a person engaged in the laudable work of extending the youthful understanding is necessitated to receive children of various and very unequal ages: amongst which number some are so well advanced as to engage and interest the master: others, again, scarce capable of lisping down the alphabet, he rarely can attend to personally because the task is irksome and unpleasant. A deputation rids him of the duty, and from the more advanced a sufficient number is selected to share the labours of the school. Whole months are now elapsed: the minor scholar is increased in size, but yet considered as too young to learn. Meanwhile has the little neglected urchin, with a probably retentive memory picked up uncouth pronunciation, in coupling the single consonants and vowels, which if ever rectified at all, will be at least a world of time and trouble.[17]

The letters and syllables drilled in the Hyde Park school were taken from the 150 copies of Dixon's *Speller* brought out by Johnson and Bain.[18] The speller of Johnson's day was a less specialised text than its modern counterpart. In addition to the abc and selected syllables, it contained prose excerpts with a religious and moralistic intent, and sections on grammar, punctuation, geography and history. Fenning's *Speller* of 1755 had dated the creation of the world at 4047 BC, Noah's flood at 2350 BC and recorded a 'very great Comet' in 1680. Sometimes the content was patriotic as in Watts's *Compleat Spelling-Book* of 1770 which paid a tribute to the establishment by a wood-cut of the unstable King George III with the verse beneath:

> In ev'ry Stroke, in ev'ry Line,
> Does some exalted Virtue shine;
> And *Albion's* Happiness we trace,
> In every Feature of his Face.[19]

Johnson's spellers were part of a package of 4,000 books put together by the SPCK and sent with the First Fleet. It comprised prayer books, psalters, testaments and Bibles, and a variety of tracts including several hundred copies of 'Plain Exhortations to Prisoners', 'Cautions to Swearers', 'Dissuasions from Stealing', 'Exercises Against Lying' and 'Exhortations to Chastity'.[20] The consignment was freighted at government expense, stored in the public store and was issued by the commissary at the chaplain's direction. The commissariat also purchased books on its own account which were distributed to the various settlements along the Australian coastline.[21]

Local supplies seldom met demand. Johnson had to wait over three years for fresh stocks of textbooks when his repeat order was sent to the inappropriate Anglican society.[22] In August 1801, missionary Rowland Hassall informed the Rev. G. Burder of the London Missionary Society that colonial schools desperately needed

... first & 2d Books as well as Spelling Books Testaments and bibles—
I have had numberless applications for the above and have given away
so that I have scarcely a Book for the Use of my own family—If you can
help me to any, they will be greatfully received—and as my son Thos is
now learning lattin—if you will be kind enough to send me any books
that will be useful to Him or myself you will do me a great favour.[23]

Three years later Hassall acknowledged receipt of

... a valuable present of Books & Tracks through from the Society. —but
beg & hope that you will still remember us in this distant sinfull nation
& let your former kind Present be only a specimin of what you will do
for us for I do ashure you that by the time the Sydney School the Parramatta Hawkesbury Toongabbie and Kissing point schools were sup-
ployed the Books were all gon, numbers of applicants was forc'd to go
without and their children perishing for lack of Knowledge, when you
send dont for get to send 2 good dictionarys 1 or 2 good Pocket Bibles,
Hymns & Supplement—[24]

A popular device of the day for economizing on spelling books
was to paste printed alphabets on to boards or cardboard and 200
sheets of these printed alphabets were sent to the colony by Mrs
Elizabeth Fry.[25] By the early 1800s spellers were on sale to the
public in the general stores but they were not available cheaply and
in quantity until a local production, based on Lindley Murray's
Spelling Book, was printed in 1810.[26]

Once the speller had been mastered, the child moved to the
primer where he could whet his reading appetite on the Creed, the
Lord's Prayer and the Ten Commandments. Eighteenth-century
school textbooks made few concessions to their child readers beyond
the occasional picture and a talking-down prose style. The standard
texts were slow to be influenced by the revolutionary layout of
Comenius's *Orbis Sensualium Pictus*, published in 1658, in which the
Moravian had attempted to relate learning to a child's interests and
abilities by blending words with pictorial representation. A general
unwillingness by pedagogues and writers to absorb radical experiments was one reason why Locke's invention of numbered and
lettered dice for classroom activities, designed to make learning 'a
sport',[27] had been rejected. Another was that it was thought likely
to encourage gambling.

Writing and arithmetic were also part of the curriculum of the
Hyde Park school. The arts of the scrivener and arithmeticker were
highly prized and a convict who practised them could charge extra
for his attainments. Such accomplishments were quite beyond the
ability of many 'abcdarians' in England where specialist schools had
opened to teach the subjects. In the writing lesson the master first

set the specimens, straight lines for the youngest, hooks and trammells for the improvers and, for advanced learners, a motto like 'Procrastination is the thief of time'. The children copied these exercises over and over again until the teacher approved their near-perfect examples.

The standard procedure in teaching arithmetic was for the teacher to work out the problems beforehand, the child then copied questions and answers down in his book. Two arithmetic texts well known in the colony were Walkinham's *Arithmetic* and Thomas Dilworth's *The Schoolmaster's Assistant*. Dilworth's started off with an introductory catechism: 'Q. What is arithmetic? A. Arithmetic is the art or science of computing by numbers, either whole or in fractions'.[28] From it the master worked the lower grades at the addition and subtraction of £s, yards, gallons and leagues, and, for the brighter child, there was the example 'What is the Root of this Squared Square-Cube 1027956394402909029176039807386?' For added variety the teacher might solve a problem from the set Dilworth had headed 'Pleasant and Diverting Questions':

> A gentleman courted a young lady, and as their birth-days happened together, they agreed to make that their wedding-day. On the day of the marriage it happened that the gentleman's age was just double to that of the lady's, that is, as 2 to 1. After they had lived together 30 years, the gentleman observed that his lady's age drew nearer to his, and that his was only in such proportion to hers as 2 to 1 3/7. Thirty years after this the same gentleman found his and his lady's ages to be as near as 2 to 1 3/5; at which time they both died.—I demand their several ages, at the day of their marriage and of their death; also the reason why the lady's age, which was continually gaining upon her husband's, should, notwithstanding, be never able to overtake it?

Arithmetic was a dull and uninteresting subject to learn. Existing practices disgusted rather than inspired pupils and one enthusiast for the subject complained in the press about the teaching methods used. 'It is not enough', Incognito argued, 'to drive into a head by main force the various tables'. The correspondent insisted that

> ... elucidation is requisite to the simplest theories, from an inattention to which, many are as little acquainted with the principles of the science after being a twelvemonth from school and out of practice, as they were when first they commenced the study.[29]

Incognito believed that a teacher had a responsibility to take his pupils further than the first four principles of arithmetic which, he assured the public, were quite insufficient to 'carry a man through life these days'. He ended his letter with a comment on multiplication whose

. . . minutiae is seldom or ever acquired until a youth, about to enter upon business, and feeling his deficiency diligently determines to surmount it; at the same time every adept must acknowledge, that the beautiful methods used in contracting its work, would equally amuse and instruct the pupil, whose curiosity by being ever kept awake would draw him imperceptibly into enquiry, and a competent knowledge of the use and power of numbers steal gradually upon the mind.[30]

Arithmetical examples taken from the few popular textbooks circulated and re-circulated among generations of pupils; and little could be done to channel the subject towards deductive reasoning until the individual method of teaching was abandoned. Not until the 1840s did textbooks appear with claims that

. . . nearly all the question being ORIGINAL, will prevent the learner from pirating answers out of other books; and it is presumed they are so varied as to prevent them from being worked mechanically and without consideration.[31]

Colonists who used the press to publicize their opinions of the aims of education were representative of educational ideas revolutionary a hundred years before. The recoiled instinctively from the soft pedagogy of Rousseau which meant for them 'the removal of restraint and the exercise of infant genius unembarrassed by the necessary awe inspired by the dictates of the preceptor'.[32] Believing as they did that every deviation from the 'true system must consequently prove injurious', their arguments stressed regularity and method as the foundation of all sound practice. By the true system, colonists were referring to the structure of the academic discipline as they knew it, while regularity and method were their synonyms for learning by regulation and rote.

When correspondents were attempting to explain what education was all about, they usually fell back on the explanatory power of the analogy. Amicus explained in a letter to *The Sydney Gazette*:

A landskip may be said to exist in a heau of colours, but the pencil of the artist must describe the scene. This allusion in the youthful mind points out the varied mass, but education is the pencil that must delineate the landskip.[33]

A more static attitude towards the nature of education was revealed by An Inquisitive Observer on 8 May 1803, when he likened the human soul without education 'to marble in a quarry, which shews none of its inherent virtues untill the skill of the polisher fetches out the colours, and discovers every ornament that lay concealed'. But by far the most popular analogy related education to the process of growth. According to Mentor, education involved the careful dissemination of 'the seeds of Virtue . . . in the infant breast',[34] which would ensure that 'the beauteous plant would spread irradicably, and the delights of Spring portend Autumnal happiness'. The comparison of education with a horticultural pursuit was considered almost certain to evoke a favourable response from an agriculturally-minded population. George Howe was responsible for this particularly fine example:

> Education is to mankind what culture is to vegetables, if this is neglected the Garden is overrun with noxious weeds; if that is forgotten the manners of men degenerate into vice and profaneness. As far, therefore, as the reasonable creature excels the vegetable, so far does education surpass agriculture. Shall a man, therefore, attend with the utmost diligence to the improvement of his ground, and neglect this far more important concern, the instruction of his offspring? Will it be pleasant or profitable for him to see his farm or his garden in high cultivation, while at the same time his children, who are to succeed him in the stage of life are indulging in idle habits or more vicious courses? We cannot surely pay too much attention to the instruction of youth.[35]

One issue of educational theory which did stir a brief controversy in the colonial press was the centuries prolonged nature *v.* nurture debate. The first protagonist was Mentor who came down on the side of the influence of the environment with a claim that 'the actions of men WHOLLY depend on the prejudices imbibed at a tender age and upon the impressions which the mind receives when in its most susceptible state'.[36] Despite his certainty, however, he did not urge that all children receive an extensive education for he believed that virtue, the goal of education, could be attained by the slightest of educational nudges. Mentor's letter brought a reply from Simplex who wanted all colonial children to receive as much schooling as they could absorb lest they slide down the moral precipice 'with fury irresistible'.[37] '*Vice*', Simplex dogmatized, invariably accompanied 'the romantic meandrings of the imagination, unguided by the torch of reason'. Those readers of *The Sydney Gazette* who expected an exposition of rival assumptions or some practical implications of the current state of the nature-nurture argument were disappointed. The rival authors paid as much attention to literary pretensions as they did to their propositions and the editor dropped the topic after two issues.

Rousseau-inspired thought in education barely stirred a ripple of controversy in New South Wales in the early 1800s. Yet by then Johann Pestalozzi had dedicated his life to introducing the irrational phenomena of trust, love and natural order into the classroom. In *How Gertrude Teaches Her Children*, published in 1801, the Swiss reformer wrote:

I wish to wrest education from the outworn order of doddering old teaching hacks as well as from the new-fangled order of cheap, artificial teaching tricks, and entrust it to the eternal powers of nature herself, to the light which God has kindled and kept alive in the hearts of fathers and mothers, to the interest of parents who desire that their children grow up in favour with God and with men.[38]

Pestalozzi believed that teaching demanded well thought-out sequences and a resort to the reality of sense impressions if it was was to be successful. His point was that 'either we go from words to things, or from things to words. Mine is the second method'.[39] Hence he wanted drawing to precede writing and reading to follow from oral exercises, and he devised lessons in which physical objects were used to stimulate ideas which the child would come to express in written form later.

Pestalozzi's theory relied on the basic postulate of Lockean philosophy which denied the existence of innate ideas. Locke had argued that ideas, derived from sensory or reflective experience, were acted upon by the mind to the extent of the individual mind's powers. Post-Lockean thinkers went on to propose that education's role was to manipulate the ideas which arose in the mind by controlling the sensory experience and that the teacher's job was to so order the external world as to permit the development of desirable ones. Some carried this argument still further by claiming that ideas could be re-organized once they had entered the mind. It was acceptance of this opinion which opened the way later in the century for the re-education theorists like D. Hartley who hypothesized that all children could be educated to think alike.

The Pestalozzian emphasis on the importance of sensations in learning provided the theoretical justification for the object lesson. But, as it happened, even the most ritualized pedagogues had nothing to fear from its introduction to the colony. It did not take schoolmen long, following their conversion to the object lesson, to translate it to their own modes of thinking which demanded an excessively mechanical treatment. Teaching through sense impressions led masters to propose formal definitions of classes of objects and to formulate strict rules for their presentation. By the second half of the nineteenth century, many object lessons were about as irrelevant a treatment of living and dead matter as man could devise.

If Johnson and his teachers were not bothered overmuch by revolutionary educational theories, they could not avoid criticism from parents. The Hyde Park classes were for the benefit of 'all Descriptions of persons, whether Soldiers, Settlers, or Convicts',[40] and some at least were soon protesting that their children were not making progress at school. Parental complaints forced the chaplain to issue a set of 'Rules or Articles to be Observed' respecting the school at Sydney, New South Wales, 1798, which was read from the pulpit at regular intervals and posted in the vestry on the governor's authority. According to the regulations parents were not to keep their children home on 'frivolous occasions' for the habit brought 'little or no Improvement in their learning, whilst the Blame is laid upon the Masters'. However, they also conceded that parents had a right to hear their children say their lessons after divine service and 'thereby see the Improvement they have made during the week'.

Eighteenth-century parents displayed little understanding of what teachers were about and teachers were equally uncertain of the role of parents in education. Dilworth thought it necessary to devote the first chapter of his arithmetic textbook, *The Schoolmaster's Assistant*, to advising teachers which parental attitudes should be encouraged and which suppressed. Parents must learn that regular attendance was the 'main axis whereon the great wheel of education turns'; that teachers' opinions should be deferred to; and that parents must be made 'sensible of their children's defects and want of parts'. It was a parent's duty to explain to his sons that 'they ought to be good boys, and learn their book and always do as their master bids them, and that if they do not, they must undergo the pain of correction'. Parents were also asked to prevent their children 'tormenting and worrying such poor animals and insects as have the misfortune to fall into their hands'. Apparently Dilworth expected the master to refer irate parents to the authority of chapter and verse and, allowing for the fact that some children would take the text home, it provided parents with a source of information of what was required of them. Another educational expert, with an eye to income above health, demanded that colonial parents allow their children no breaks from study arguing that once a child had 'entered the lists of improvement', parental duty required the enforcement of attendance

> . . . without impediment or interruption, as holidays not only check the progress of their study, but render the task of the teachers irksome, the temper of the pupil sullen and perverse; for a relish for idleness once imbibed, cannot be removed, if at all, without fatigue to the one, and pain and regret to the other.[41]

The disparate and inappropriate demands put upon the child were the root cause of the eighteenth-century schoolmaster's unending disciplinary problems. The children in the Hyde Park school were punished for 'swearing, lying, stealing, or any other ill or wicked Habit' in the belief that it would make them good; but, if after 'such Punishment as the Masters (first acquainting Mr Johnson with the Crime and having his concurrence) shall think proper to inflict', no reformation was effected, the offender was to be 'turned from school'.[42] Johnson made it quite clear that attendance at his school was not theirs by right but was a 'Privilege' and 'Benefit'.

A common punishment in colonial school and society was a flogging. Once Johnson stopped a master's allowance for treating his scholars 'too severely'[43] and for frequent intoxication; however, his apparently well-founded charges were insufficient in themselves to stop parents from sending their children to his school. Corporal punishment had an accepted place in the educational theory of the day. It was used to counter weakness of memory and slowness of apprehension, and its application was thought to build character. The floggers had a luke-warm ally in Locke who, though he thought corporal punishment the last resort, advocated its use for 'obstinancy, which is an open defiance'[44] and for putting down schoolroom rebellions. The philosopher illustrated his stand by reference to a personal experience:

> A prudent and kind mother of my acquaintance was, on such an occasion, forced to whip her little daughter, at her first coming home from from nurse eight times successively the same morning, before she could master her stubborness, and obtain a compliance in a very easy and indifferent matter. If she had left off sooner, and stopped at the seventh whipping, she had spoiled the child forever, and, by her unprevailing blows, only confirmed her refractoriness, very hardly afterwards to be cured: but wisely persisting till she had bent her mind, and suppled her will, the only end of correction and chastisement, she established her authority thoroughly in the very first occasions, and had ever after a very ready compliance and obedience in all things from her daughter; for as this was the first time, so I think it was the last time too she ever struck her.[45]

Severity was a virtue for the eighteenth-century teacher. One methodical German estimated that he had administered 1,035,537 strokes with rod and cane in his fifty years of teaching, apart from inflicting other punishments like forcing children to kneel on peas and hold up rods.[46] In American schools beatings were administered to children with ferule, rattan, cow-hide, and even a cat-o'-nine-tails;[47] and there were the ingenious devices of a split wood for a recalcitrant pupil's nose and the dunce's cap for the classroom's lying Ananias. One school at Sunderland, Massachusetts, had a whipping-post set in the floor and its walls were marked by the dents of canes thrown by generations of teachers.

The prevalence of corporal punishment must be set in the context of the age in which the extremes of child punishments saw the confinement of malefactory pupils in fetters and the hanging of minors with the display of their bodies on gibbets. Many applied the rod unsparingly in their attempts to bend a child's mind to the correct shape, to shock him out of idleness and to put down class-room insurrections. 'A boy has a back; when you hit it he understands' was a dictum familiar to eighteenth-century teachers. The point is worth making though, that for all the deficiencies in his teachers, methods and equipment, the kindly Johnson and his ex-convict teachers ran their school without resort to the ingenuity of those Englishmen at home who hauled offenders to the ceiling in iron cages or who taught their classes against the backdrop of a hangman's scaffold.[48]

Chapter VI

THE ADMINISTRATION OF COLONIAL SCHOOLS

> . . . as much has been done as it was possible
> —All confidence for some years has been at
> an end between me and the Governor. It
> required no common caution to get as much
> done for the schools as have been done. I
> could only move in the Back Ground.
>
> MARSDEN to J. T. BIGGE[1]

The antagonism which Marsden represented in his dealings with Macquarie was typical of the relations between governor and chaplain before 1825. While leadership in public education alternated between the two offices and was fully effective only when they cared to co-operate, conflicts between them often frustrated plans for education. The causes of their disputes went deeper than personalities bearing as they did on the tension between the temporal and spiritual in a colony where the power of the state's chief executive was unmatched. Where deficiencies in schooling were the direct outcome of these rivalries then the governor must carry most blame for the final responsibility was his.

Government in New South Wales was essentially a military administration. That this was intentional may be gathered by the omission from Phillip's Instructions of any authority to summon a council or assembly, a clause commonly found in the papers of the governors of other Crown colonies. In effect New South Wales was ruled as if it were the fo'c'sle of a man-o'-war or the head station of a slave plantation. The governor issued all daily orders excepting only battalion orders, he scrutinized the criminal and magistrates' procedures revising them where he thought fit, fixed rations and prices, granted permission to marry, authorized assistance to settlers and controlled the disposition of public labour. All magistrates were appointed by him. He had powers to pardon and reprieve, levy armed forces, proclaim martial law, erect fortifications, direct finance and commerce, and to dispense land grants.[2] The military and civil officers including the chaplains were his subordinates and, beneath them again, was a lower class whose members whether freemen, convicts or private soldiers had a minimum of judicial rights and no political representation whatever.

Nevertheless the governor was no oriental despot. His authority was restrained by a Crown commission for he was ultimately responsible to his superiors in England and was liable to be sued for acts in excess of his lawful authority.[3] But by far the most significant practical restriction of his sovereignty was his need for a *modus vivendi* with the colonial *élite*. Here the governor was dependent on the good-will of the military and the close co-operation of his civil establishment which included a private secretary, deputy-judge advocate, surveyor, commissary, chaplain, and a surgeon-general with three assistants. Although these men were civil appointees, in effect they acted the role of subordinate staff officers for by virtue of their commissions they were subject to 'the rules and discipline of war'.[4]

The three offices having most contact with teachers were the governor's secretary later known as the colonial secretary, the commissary and the chaplain. All requests for aid for schools and the appointment of public schoolmasters passed through the hands of the colonial secretary who referred them to the governor for decision. Once a teacher had joined the establishment, it fell to the commissary to issue his rations, firewood and slops. But it was the chaplain who provided him with his closest contact with officialdom. Schools were established, maintained and the content of schooling determined under his guidance. Nonetheless a colonial chaplain still required the governor's consent for all his important executive actions, a dependence in marked contrast with contemporary practice in England where the rights of the church in education were recognized if not universally approved.

The unique place of the Church of England in New South Wales was acknowledged in 1786 when the salary item of 10s. a day[5] was added to the staffing establishment to pay for a chaplain. The ministry went to the Rev. Richard Johnson, a recent graduate of Magdalene College, Cambridge, on the recommendation of members of the Eclectic Society, a group of evangelical clergy which included Wilberforce, the poet William Cowper and the philanthropist John Thornton. Whether this early appointment of a chaplain argues for the establishment of the Church of England in law in New South Wales seems unlikely, although the status of the colonial church certainly went beyond that of a transient military chaplaincy. In his Instructions, Phillip had been ordered to 'take such steps for the due celebration of publick worship as circumstances will permit',[6] and he was directed to set land aside for glebes for the Church of England. Again at the Select Committee on Transportation of 1812, the ex-governors were cross-examined at length about the condition in which they had left 'the established Church'[7] in New South Wales. For their part, the early governors expressed no hesitations in making policy for 'the established church of this colony'.[8] Their certainty regarding the bond between church and state was best demonstrated when King deliberately named the colony's first parishes St (Arthur) Phillip and St John (Hunter).[9]

The working rule of establishment was not followed up by any legal codification of rights from England. The Church of England hierarchy there seldom bothered itself with the affairs of its colonial priests. Indeed there was uncertainty as to who the ecclesiastical superiors of the local chaplains actually were. Johnson considered himself the subordinate of the Bishop of London, but that the association between colonial priest and hierarchy was tenuous was indicated when the same Bishop repudiated any ecclesiastical juris-diction over Marsden and by the refusal of the Archbishop of Canterbury to intervene directly in that chaplain's bitter disputes with Macquarie.[10] Reinforcements from home for the two pioneering priests were slow to arrive. In Phillip's governorship, the church had approved the appointment of Rev. J. Crowther but the priest turned back after being shipwrecked off Table Bay.[11] While an attempt by the missionary branch to recruit the Rev. C. Haddock also aborted when the man drew his colonial settling-in allowance but remained in England.[12] There was to be no infusion for the colonial church until 1809 when the first of two priests recruited by Marsden disembarked.

Johnson's appointment as chaplain delighted the homeside evangelicals who had encouraged him to try for the post. Rev. H. Venn surmised that under his pastoral care the 'lost creatures' of Botany Bay would 'steal no more';[13] while the converted slave-trader Rev. J. Newton was confident that historians would come to rank Johnson above 'Colombus, Drake and Cook'.[14] However, the chaplain's allegiance to evangelical theology did not endear him to colonists in high places. Conversions at this time were commonly experienced by the English working class and, so far as many of their betters were concerned, enthusiasm was not yet respectable. The upper class still preferred the orthodoxy of 'a quiet and some-what lazy Church',[15] to wrestling with the Devil, encounters with hell-fire or a rigorous Sunday observance. Wilberforce referred scathingly to the heresies that man was naturally good though prone to error and which regarded the Devil as 'an evanescent prejudice which it would now be to the discredit of any man of understanding to believe', as John Bull's 'rational religion'.[16]

Fancying 'less doctrinal teaching, and more plain exhortation to honest purpose in life,'[17] Phillip had taken exception to the content of Johnson's sermons before the Fleet left Plymouth. The chaplain's sponsors then urged him to try for a balance between 'a dry detail of doctrines and a dry enforcement of moral duties',[18] but he had little success in finding middle ground. Johnson's reaction to their advice was to begin preaching 'awfully' and he had to be reminded that 'To persons in this state, denunciations of wrath too frequently repeated, instead of working savingly upon them, rather tends to increase the enmity of their minds against God'.[19] Others had less patience. They stigmatized Johnson by the name Methodist[20] and so helped destroy the chaplain's religious credibility among more orthodox churchmen.

For Johnson and his young bride the passage out was marked by services to unresponsive congregations unmoved by the priest's choice of sermons like 'the heinous evil of *common* swearing'[21] which he preached at Rio. More discouraging still was the lack of official confidence that he would achieve widespread religious conversions. The signs were there when the governor determined that the events of the first Sunday left no time for a pause for divine service and when the chaplain had no option but to hold his service in the shade of some trees on the second. In 1791 the foundations for a church were dug at Parramatta but before the building could be completed it was converted into a gaol and eventually became a granary.[22] During Phillip's governorship, Johnson preached in a partially erected storehouse and, when this neared completion, he was moved to the barracks, then to a carpenter's shop and finally to an old boat house. Johnson claimed that his health suffered from ministering in makeshift premises and he averred in 1792 that he had been more comfortable and certain of his venue under his tree four years before.[23] The obvious unwillingness of the authorities to build him a permanent church was remarked on by a priest from the Spanish fleet visiting Port Jackson in 1793:

> The priest belonging to the Commodore's ship, on observing that there was not any church built, lifted up his eyes with astonishment, and declared, that had the place been settled by his nation, a house for God would have been erected before any house for man.[24]

Johnson attributed the falling off in his congregation to the accommodation provided 'sometimes no one-half, one-third, and sometimes one-fourth of the convicts (especially the women) present'.[25] For whatever reason, their response to his preaching was such that he preferred to visit a few chosen convicts in their huts rather than face them *en masse* from the pulpit. Understandably

the chaplain's sense of vocation faltered among people who 'will
sell their souls for a Glass of Grogg'. 'Most', he declared, 'wd rather
see a Tavern, a Play House, a Brothel—anything sooner than a
place for publick worship'.[26]

If Johnson's relationship with Phillip can be described as one of
covert hostility, then the term persecution could apply to his
situation under the acting governor Major F. Grose. Johnson was
relieved of his magistracy when Grose took command and the chaplain charged the military with deliberately obstructing his religious
duties shortly afterwards. He complained that an officer had inter-
rupted divine service by ordering the fall-out drum beat—'instantly
the corps took their arms, got into their ranks, and marched away.
I had then been barely three-quarters of an hour in the whole
service, and was then about the middle of my discourse!'[27] Johnson
was sufficiently upset to write to Secretary of State Dundas explaining
that, although well aware 'of the subordinate station I hold in the
colony under Major Grose as the Lieutenant-Governor',[28] he had
no option but to lodge an official complaint when he went without
a sexton, grave-digger or an official parish clerk. His grievances also
provoked him to write to the Archbishop of Canterbury alleging
that ecclesiastical matters were 'not at all attended to' in the
colony.[29]

In 1793 Grose had been reminded from Whitehall that 'whatever
tends to increase the respect for the clerical station and character is
highly important and necessary on all occasions'.[30] Instead of
achieving its desired effect apparently the major conceived the
recommendation as reflecting on his administration. Grose smeared
the chaplain with the label Methodist 'is a very troublesome, discon-
tented character'[31] claiming he would have reported him at headquarters except for pity of his large family. Johnson, however, had
the last word. In a sermon preached on the Sunday following
Governor Hunter's arrival, Johnson spent upwards of an hour
in the pulpit exposing the social evils of the last government 'their
extortion, their despotism, their debauchery and ruin of the colony,
driving it almost to famine by the sale of liquors at 1,200 per cent.
profit'.[32] The chaplain concluded by congratulating colonists on the
abolition of the military government and on the restoration of the
rule of law.

Johnson's subordinate position in the colonial administration can
be gauged from the fact that the places and times of his services were
determined for him by the governor and that he was once refused
permission to visit prisoners awaiting execution.[33] However the
chaplain was not prepared to be a martyr of anybody else's making.
For consolation he turned to farming and the successful cultivation

of orange trees, cabbages, turnips, water melon, limes, strawberries and tobacco. In this way he built a life for himself and his family, which included two Aboriginal girls and the two orphaned Lee children, in the company of the other outcasts from government house.

As was the case with some of his ecclesiastical duties, the super-intendence of colonial schools did not fall to Johnson by virtue of his office. It was very much a delegated duty. That he had 'pro-posed'[34] to the governor that two women be appointed school-teachers indicates that the chaplain was not in the position to make the decision himself; nor could he be certain that Chaplain Bain would be appointed supervisor of the Norfolk Island teacher, Thomas McQueen.[35] Johnson also required the governor's prior con-sent before he was able to accept SPG money for his schools. This indeterminate role of the chaplaincy in colonial education was appreciated in England where Wilberforce thought it quite proper to nominate marine officer Lt W. Dawes for the post of superinten-dent of colonial school regardless of the fact that the man was not in holy orders.[36]

The restricted opportunity for Johnson to act effectively in education was demonstrated when he found himself unable to sack Webster, the punitive schoolmaster of the New South Wales Corps. In 1796 Johnson advised the directors of the SPG not to pay the corporal the £30 they owed him because he was 'too much addicted to drinking' and treated his pupils too harshly.[37] 'Most of the chil-dren', the chaplain explained, 'have been taken from him, & several of them sent to Richardson'. But Johnson's disapproval did not go with the power to dismiss the corporal who continued to teach his school under the protection of the military until he left the colony in 1803,[38] a man of some renown having the street Webster's Row, named after him.[39]

Johnson has been credited with the initiation of the first colonial schools. This mantle appears to have fallen on him by way of the expectation that, in this age, education and religion invariably occured together. But if Isabella Rosson did keep her school in 1789 then it was unlikely to have been at the chaplain's instigation. In 1792 Johnson wrote home that things were 'in an unsettled confused state, on which account it was impossible to get any schools erected or established', and that he had just suggested

. . . to his Excellency to have a person appointed at different places to instruct them to read—To this he readily consented, & myself was appointed to superintend them—we have now one school established at *Sydney* & another at *Parramatta*.—a schoolmistress appointed for each.[40]

Of course Isabella may not have opened her school as early as 1798. The evidence that she did so rests on her husband's testimony taken at the Select Committee on Transportation of 1812. Perhaps Richardson misled the chairman to give him a better impression of himself by his choice of a schoolmistress as a bride; or his memory may have played him false. However, there is a later comment from Johnson which notes that both the Richardsons were teaching 'about the beginning of the year Ninety'.[41] This, when taken with the chaplain's comment on the chaotic state of the colony before 1792, argues that Isabella's school did in fact pre-date his own efforts.

While the popular assertion that Johnson *'alone* did anything for the education of the children'[42] is mistaken, by 1792 he had two women teaching at Sydney and Parramatta and had already made representations in England to widen the scope of colonial education. Johnson wanted classes to open for those convicts 'as wished & wanted, to be instructed to read';[43] and he proposed that these be held on Sunday 'in a way not to interfere with publick work'. In making his pleas the chaplain reassured his reader that the measure would cost 'a very little pittance'. However, no support was forthcoming for the plan or for a request he made at the same time for two missionaries to come out to teach Aboriginal children.

Little is known of Johnson's educational philosophy. Possibly it was influenced by his Moravian religious sympathies, certainly his encouragement of hymn singing paralleled their practices. The model Moravian school was run by Count Zinzendorf at a settlement near Dresden. Zinzendorf taught from Bible extracts translated into the modern idiom, and he attempted to reveal Christ to the child 'as clearly as he can see a house'[44] using activity teaching methods and by working children in groups. There is no evidence though that Johnson had any direct contact with Herrnhut.

A peak year for Johnson was 1798 when he had three masters teaching close to 200 children in his temporary church. After the building was fired, enrolments halved and the chaplain determined to return home quite possibly for good. Marsden's portrait of him on his departure in 1800 was of a man 'brought to the Verge of the Grave . . . exhausted with Toil, vexation & privations'.[45] Back home Johnson found that little attention was paid to ex-colonial chaplains. After his salary was exhausted he worked as a curate until a friend's kindness brought him a rectorship in the City of London. By then, according to Marsden, it was too late to benefit him much 'as he had lost from the decay of his natural Strength and Spirits all that warmth Zeal and Energy which are so very essential to make a minister useful and acceptable to his People'. Yet it must be admitted that Johnson sold part of his property in New South Wales for the considerable sum of £400 and that he was a wealthy man when he died at the ripe age of seventy-four.

Marsden is remembered in many guises: as a priest who put business first; a privileged citizen seeking to impose his reactionary notions of class on egalitarian New South Welshmen; a clerical politician working insidiously against the public good; and a parson-magistrate addicted to flogging. Yet opposed to these assessments stands a minority opinion which respects him as the apostle of Maoriland, a humanitarian noted for his generosity to colonists of all social classes, and a man with a name for 'prudence, activity, intrepidity, and piety'.[46] Most of these conflicting reputations can be traced back to the acrimonious controversies of a long chaplaincy, the bitterness and rancour of which spilled over into the administration of colonial education.

Young Marsden attended the village school at Farsley, Yorkshire, before he was apprenticed to a blacksmith; and, when his district came under the influence of the Methodist revival, the youthful craftsman joined the Leeds Methodist Society. Marsden took up lay preaching in his district with a forthrightness which drew him to the attention of the Elland Society, an evangelical church group whose members gave him the opportunity of returning to school preparatory to entering the ministry. He is said to have prepared himself for university entrance by chalking Latin declensions on the fireboard of his forge.[47] Enrolled at Hull Grammar School, the acolyte met the Milner brothers and Wilberforce and he was in residence at Magdalene College, Cambridge, when the patronage of the Society secured him the vacant assistant chaplaincy of New South Wales. Marsden did not wait to take out a degree. By May 1793 he was ordained and two months later the Marsdens were aboard the *William* on their way to Botany Bay. Following a brief period at Norfolk Island, the couple returned to the mainland to settle permanently at Parramatta.

No church was ready for Marsden in the Parramatta district and he counted himself lucky to find a convict hut in which to shelter his congregations. In his first six months of preaching, the chaplain admitted to having turned up only two in two thousand colonists with 'the smallest concern for their souls';[48] at this point he was forced to concede that it was a matter of some doubt with him whether 'His Power will be ever seen in this place to fall like Lightning from Heaven'. Then there was personal tragedy to contend with. Two of his young sons were killed, one thrown from his mother's arms in a gig accident and the other scalded to death. At the end of his first decade in New South Wales circumstances had brought Marsden to the belief that:

I shall be happy should I ever live to see religion flourish amongst us. There is no prospect of this. I often think the Gospel, if we may judge from appearances in this settlement, was only intended for children, the common soldier and the convict in irons.[49]

Marsden's experiences with the colony's governing *élite* were as unsatisfactory as his predecessor's had been. He depicted his superiors as 'Unconverted men in power' roaring 'like lions at the sound of the Gospel', all 'lost to God and Religion'.[50] So far as their system of government went, Marsden thought it best understood through a study of the principles of absolutism.

Absolute Power will always have a Tendency to corrupt the human mind—an Admiral or a General from the nature of their Profession, cannot enter into the views of a Clergyman, can form no Judgement what is duties to his People are; and their arbitrary Conduct is so repugnant to his ideas of civil and religious Liberty, that his Feelings are much more wounded at their harsh Language, than they otherwise would have been, if Custom in early Life had made him familiar with despotic Power.[51]

Yet life in New South Wales had its compensations above those he had known as an artisan in England. Accepting the Calvinist doctrine that a man should not bury his talent, Marsden yoked holiness and *bourgeois* efficiency together to secure the reputation of the colony's 'best practical farmer'.[52] He became adviser to the government on wool production and sent sample fleeces home to the Royal Society. In 1804 the cleric worked 1,720 acres which included plots of maize, barley, oats, vegetables and an orchard; he grazed 1,210 sheep and 34 cattle; and kept 97 hogs, 19 goats and 12 horses.[53] On his visit to England in 1807, Marsden had a suit made up from his own wool which he wore at an audience with George III. The king admired the cloth so much that he had a coat made from the same clip and presented the assistant chaplain with a gift of five pure-bred merino ewes.[54] By 1812 Marsden had an English market for 4000 lbs of wool at 45d. per lb.[55]

His business acumen brought its accompanying embarrassments not solely because of the principle involved, for had not the Archbishop of Canterbury recommended that the he receive a £50 grant for farming implements and seeds before he set out,[56] but also his remarkable success upset the critics. In a statement to Commissioner J.T. Bigge made in 1821, Marsden defended himself against charges that he had neglected the spiritual concerns of his parish to further his private business ventures:

. . . I enter a Country in a State of nature where the ground has never been subdued by the Mattock or the Hoe—If I wanted a Cabbage or a

Potatoe I must plant them with my own hands—If I wanted a Bushel of Wheat I must grow it or starve—I had never one given me since I have been in the Colony nor so much as a Barn Door Fowl—This is not the case in England. The Clergy have often the first Fruits of the Earth here they have none. My fees for 14 years did not exceed £1 pr annum. I was also placed in the centre of Felons that neither regarded me nor my preaching generally. And if by my own manual Labour I raised a Cabbage or Potatoe they would steal it from me. It was not from Inclination that either The Revd. Richd. Johnstone or myself in the infant state of the Colony took the Axe, the Spade and the Hoe—We could not help ourselves and we thought it no disgrace to labor—St. Paul's own hands ministered to his wants in a cultivated nation—Ours in an uncultivated one and should this be cast upon us as a reproach— If it is a Reproach it ought not to fall upon us—Our Country ought either to have made a suitable provision for us or not to blame us if we laboured to supply our real necessities when exiled from our native Country and Friends—[57]

The other major argument used by Marsden in his attempts to justify his activities centred on his contribution to the growth of a colonial wool industry. 'Many think nothing of these things now', he wrote to a close friend in England. 'They cannot see any advantage to be derived to them, their children, or this settlement by improving the fleeces of our Sheep. But I anticipate immense natural wealth to spring from this source of Commerce in time'.[58] When he issued his prophecy Marsden admitted that he could well be 'too fond of the garden, the field and the fleece', but he felt obliged to point out that civilization and cultivation were the harbingers of greater blessings and that he was following the Biblical injunction of beating swords into plough shares and spears into pruning hooks.

Marsden's practical outlook came through strongly in his ideas on education. He thought a Church of England schooling essential if colonial children were not to walk 'in the footsteps of their wretched parents: the boys will be idle and rebellious, and the girls infamous . . . the former living by plundering the industrious, and the latter by prostitution'.[59] It was the populace, he warned, who would have to pay for such 'mischief' which would cost 'a great expenditure of public money' to set aright. According to Marsden, antisocial behaviour in youth could be countered by making education compulsory. In turn this was possible only if the government were persuaded to mount a vigorous recruitment programme for teachers 'of tolerable education and good morals'. Although not all of his aims were achieved, in the early years of Macquarie's governorship several charity day schools opened in the new townships and Marsden was able to write home:

The rising generation are now under education in almost all parts of the country. The Catholic priests have all left us, so that we have now the whole field to ourselves. I trust much good will be done; some amongst us are turning to the Lord. Our Churches are well attended, which is promising and encouraging to us. My colleagues are men of piety and four of the schoolmasters. This will become a great country in time, it is much favoured in its soil and climate.[60]

Proselytism in the name of the name of the Church of England was a legitimate aim and an important goal of education for Marsden who was apprehensive for the future should Roman Catholicism be countenanced officially. He predicted that New South Wales would be 'lost to the British Empire in less than one year' should this happen.[61] His main suggestion to avoid the calamity was to urge that Church of England men and women marry Roman Catholics and send their children to the public schools. Without the example of Anglican spouses, he believed the colony's Roman Catholics could never slough off their tribal Irishness. Marsden put the Irish convicts in the category of

> . . . the lowest class of the Irish nation; who are the most wild, ignorant and savage race that were ever favoured with the Light of Civilization; men that have been familiar with Robberies, Murders and every horrid Crime from their Infancy. Their minds being destitute of every Principle of religion and Morality render them capable of perpetrating the most nefarious Acts in cool Blood. As they never appear to reflect upon Consequences, but to be governed entirely by the Impulse of Passion, and always alive to rebellion and mischief, they are very dangerous members of society . . . they are extremely superstitious artful and treacherous . . .[62]

The chaplain asserted that Irish convicts would not object to the baptism of their children at Anglican ceremonies for, although they professed to be Roman Catholics, he believed that they had 'very little knowledge or regard for any religion'. When the practice of church baptism and schooling became widespread, Marsden was certain that Roman Catholicism would become extinct in the colony and that the next generation would come to attach itself cheerfully to the government. Although he credited the force of education with accelerating the process of social amelioration, the chaplain was realist enough to appreciate that family stability had a prior claim, arguing that in a society which tolerated concubinage, the best of educational reforms must fail. Marsden was adamant that 'without matrimony, no instruction given by the schoolmasters, no labours of the clergy, no power of the executive authority can render any moral and religious advantage to the rising generation'.[63]

Usually the colony's non-conformists and the chaplains of the Church of England worked well together. Marsden helped the stranded missionaries of the London Missionary Society settle into colonial life with gifts of food, by advice on investing their money in 'four feet' and through private loans, and for others he found government or private employment. In encouraging his congregations to join him in singing Methodist hymns, Marsden was displaying that tolerance of marginal differences in Protestant doctrine which led one dissenter churchman to describe him as a man in whom 'there was no bigotry'.[64] The chaplain's openly-displayed hatred of Roman Catholicism was no bar to this opinion either for many Protestants considered the Pope and the Anti-Christ of the prophets one and the same thing.

For all his tolerance, Marsden reacted vehemently when dissenter interference threatened the traditional privileges of the church. He played a part in the eviction of missionary Crook from a Hawkesbury public school when the over-zealous man celebrated communion from unconsecrated household dishes.[65] Again, when a group of dissenters introduced Sunday schools to Parramatta in competition with Anglican teaching, Marsden and Macquarie acting for once in concert closed them.[66] The chaplain claimed that Sunday schools had no place in New South Wales where

> . . . There are no manufactories yet here for the employment of the children, and the benevolence of the British Government has provided for the Instruction of the poorer classes in the week days.—The collecting of the children on the Sabbath Day to the Public Schools, has been with a view more to induce Habits of Morality and respect for the Sabbath, and the Divine Ordinances, than to learn them to read.[67]

Although his argument had point, the chaplain obviously feared that children would be poached from the public schools. The dispute was reminiscent of events in England where the early union of church and dissent in founding Sunday schools failed to survive fears of the inroads of French revolutionary thought with non-Anglican teachers being seen as disseminators of 'Jacobinical principles of sedition and atheism'.[68]

The appointment of the LMS missionary, William Shelley, as manager of the Black Native Institution in 1815 provided another example of a situation where Marsden thought himself and his church slighted. While the chaplain owned a property next door to the BNI, he never cared to visit it.[69] Indeed Shelley's very idea cut across one of the chaplain's theories which postulated the ineducability of Aborigines through European-type schooling. Marsden believed that the discipline of hard work must precede conversion, an opinion reinforced when he failed in attempts to civilize an Aboriginal boy who waited at his table. The chaplain's attitude towards the Aborigines contrasted with his efforts on behalf of the sons of Maori chieftans. For these children Marsden found money in England for a school at Parramatta although he was forced to close it in 1822 after thirteen of the inmates had died.[70]

Other contributions by Marsden to colonial education in the period before 1810 were the time and money he spent on the female orphan school, the five salaried posts for clergymen and school-teachers which he extracted from the British treasury, and, equally as important, his recruitment of the men to take them up. On a personal level, public schoolmaster John Eyre has left a record of the chaplain's association with his school at Parramatta:

> The Rev. Mr. Marsden very frequently came into the School after the Evening Service, and addressed the children in a very plain and familiar manner: sometimes on parts of the sermon of the day and at times improving some particular recent occurrence, the children paying considerable attention. He also gave them yearly, for many years at his own expense, a pleasant repast at the School, or at his house, which had a good effect on the minds of the children and parents: and before they were dismissed their pleasant regalements he gave them a short discourse and sung a hymn.[71]

This unostentatious kindness which Marsden often acted out in private bears little relation to the exaggerated public utterances for which he is better known. Typical of these was his sermon on the quality of colonial life returned by an English publisher with the comment 'the scenes described are so shocking that I fear their very description might tend to excite ideas in multitudes which would be better never known'.[72]

Educational activities absorbed only a fraction of Marsden's abundant energies. Apart from the demands of his business ventures and the oversight of police and government works at Parramatta, he had continuous and exacting duties on the bench.

> . . . there being no magistrate but myself at Parramatta, nor in any of the Districts from the South Creek to Kissing Point and Concord. The whole of the Complaints in these remote & extensive districts, South Creek, Seven Hills, Baulkham Hill, Castle Hill, etc., etc., came before me as a Single Magistrate.[73]

There are indications that Marsden was an unwilling law-giver in the early days,[74] but soon he came to prize his appointment highly arguing that the clerical magistracy was an essential of good government. In practising his beliefs the chaplain gained an unenviable reputation for general severity. The extremes to which they

led him were demonstrated at the time of the Castlehill rebellion
when he was party to the flogging of a convict in an attempt to
extract a confession.[75] Remembering that clerical justices were
common at the time in England, it is still difficult not to share something of Rev. Dr J.D. Lang's condemnation:

> In other countries the clergy have often been accused of taking the *fleece;*
> but New South Wales is the only country I have ever heard of in which
> they are openly authorized, under a royal commission, to take the *hide*
> also, or to flay the flock alive.[76]

The reputation of Marsden suffers from his over-ready acceptance
of many harsh conventions of a penal settlement. But the attitudes
which some so readily condemned in him, his acute sense of property
and of the protection of property, were not Marsden's exclusively
being uppermost in the thinking of many of his religious and
'ungodly'[77] contemporaries. Unlike the chaplain though, not all of
these men could boast a second face for the world.

> . . . the Revd. Mr. Marsden hath also engaged to preach at Kissing
> Point on the first wensday evening of every Month & acted accordingly.
> I believe he hath the work of God at heart & with unweared zeal he goes
> on with the new Church in Parramatta & what with is Public situation
> (as heald superintendent of these Settelements as well as J.P.) the church
> & the orphan school he hath enough to do on a Sunday he preaches at
> Sydney in the Morning & Parramatta in the Afternoon, is Diligence in
> the above does him Much Credit.[78]

In arguing Marsden's case, note should be taken of an address presented to him in 1807 by the Hawkesbury settlers which thanked
him for his community services as minister, magistrate and inspector
of all 'Public, Orphan and Charity Schools'.[79] Four pages of
signatures follow.

Both Johnson and Marsden ministered in days when the governors
of New South Wales conceived the church to be an appendage of
their military-style administrations. Provided they give their chaplains opportunities to preach, they considered their obligations
met. Not until 1810 did a governor concede that his senior chaplain
had any authority over the assistant chaplains, while the chaplain's
power over the teachers he superintended was less certain even than
this. When two public schoolteachers criticized Marsden's administration of education in 1817, he could only threaten that as he was
a member of the orphan school committee they were 'in a certain
way'[80] his subordinates. This severely restricted authority of the
chaplain's office in educational matters was still evident in 1822
when Rev. R. Hill advertised a vacancy for a schoolmaster in *The
Sydney Gazette*. Brisbane directed that he take no further action

beyond returning all tenders to his office[81] and he went on to put a nominee of his own in the £100-per-annum post. In the absence of close support from the governors, colonial chaplains could achieve little in education. Similarly the spasms of interest which the governors themselves showed in schooling required the willing attachment of the clergy for their continuity. The happy state of a conjunction of interests was rarely attained.

Chapter VII

MISSIONARY CONTRIBUTORS
TO COLONIAL EDUCATION

. . . there is one branch of duty however of
peculiar importance for the discharge of
which we hope most of you are qualified—
& which is equally incumbent on the
preacher and the Lay brother. We refer to
the education and religious instruction of the
children both of the Convicts, and of the
poor Colonists, and of as many of the native
heathens as you can procure & attend to—
in this great duty the Women also may be of
peculiar Use and altho' an assiduous attention to this employment may be less grati-
fying than public preaching—it is no less
necessary, and may in its consequences be as
beneficial; and as it implies more self-denial,
patience, and humility—it affords at least as
fair a proof of the true Missionary Spirit—
this subject is in our estimation so very
important that we not only press it on your
attention, but desire you will inform Us in
all your letters what progress you make
therein—

DIRECTORS of LMS
to Port Jackson Missionaries, 1799[1]

In 1798 internecine warfare drove eleven missionaries of the London
Missionary Society and their families from the island paradise of
Tahiti to seek refuge in the squalid penal settlement of New South
Wales. The decision which several of them made to take up teaching
for a living put an end to the working monopoly of convicts and
ex-convicts in public schools and Anglican chaplains were required
to supervise independent non-conformist schoolmasters for the first
time. Doctrinal differences between chaplain and missionary may
not appear worth commenting upon in a colony whose clergy
professed broad evangelical sympathies and where most congregations assembled because they had to. However, one outcome of the

induction of dissenters into the ranks of the public schoolmasters was to make uniformity in religious education more difficult to achieve in the years ahead. When the *Nautilus* berthed though, all this was in the future. The exiles were warmly welcomed by men who valued the injection of their skills into the workforce, by others who anticipated the beneficial effect on society of an active Protestant mission, and by a very few motivated by thoughts of companionship with people for whom the religious life mattered.

The missionaries were witness to a revival of militant Christianity in the Pacific where conversion had lanquished since the heyday of the Spanish and Portugese in the Phillipines and the East Indies. Even in those days, the influence of Roman Catholicism and of the Russian clergy out of Kamchatka was sporadic so far as most Pacific islanders were concerned. For them the coming of Christianity dated almost entirely from the nineteenth century. This most recent Pacific excursion was part of a world-wide movement which took its inspiration from the evangelical revival. By the early 1790s, the Wesleyan Missionary Society was operating in the West Indies and the Baptist Missionary Society had sent a man to India; and it was not long before the Edinburgh and the Church Missionary Societies joined them by establishing overseas missions of their own. As a result of these endeavours, Protestant evangelism penetrated the Indies, Ceylon, the Cape Colony, Australia and China by the mid-century.

The LMS which backed the Port Jackson missionaries, was very much part of this Protestant crusade. Its genesis was an appeal from a 'powerfully acted upon' Dr Bogue in 1794,[2] printed in the *Evangelical Magazine* founded the year previously 'to stem the torrent of ungodliness', in which the doctor urged his readers to unite in a mission to disseminate evangelical truth among the unenlightened nations. The new Society had the support of the chaplain to the Countess of Huntingdon, the enthusiastic Rev. Dr Haweis, who directed its attention to the South Seas by his 'enchanting' picture[3] of evangelical opportunities there. Already Haweis had failed in attempts to have three missionaries sail with Bligh and in the recruitment of two men for island preaching when the Bishop of London refused to ordain his choices—they were not university men.[4] Haweis was to achieve his ends through the LMS whose directors, aided by a £500 donation from the chaplain, purchased the *Duff* and accepted the offer of the competent seaman Captain James Wilson to sail her to Tahiti free of charge.

The directors knew well that Tahiti stood in need of evangelizing. Details of Pacific island life were well-known in England from the publication of Captain James Cook's *Voyages* and Joseph Bank's papers; and there were the equally popular if once-removed re-enactments of the theatre, romanticized sketches and paintings, and accounts in novels. To upper-class Englishmen, Tahiti was an exciting place of great scientific interest, a source of intriguing anthropological speculation; but to the lower-class artisans who were the strength of the LMS, this was Satan's kingdom where infanticide, human sacrifice and homosexuality went unrestrained by any saving notion of Protestant guilt.

Although the LMS proclaimed its non-denominationalism and included Church of England clergy and laymen among its organizers, the affiliation of the *Duff* recruits came closest to fundamental Calvinism. They accepted predestination, preached the atonement and the reality of conversion, and when one of their party was suspected of the Arminian heresy he was promptly excommunicated.[5] Ordained men among them were not to enjoy any special privileges while links with the state were specifically debarred in a statement which all signed affirming that 'There is no other head of the church but the Lord Jesus Christ; neither hath any temporal prince, secular power, or civil magistrate, any right to exercise any authority over her'.[6] For inspiration then, the missionaries looked to the logic of Calvinism rather than to the simple Moravianism of Johnson or the broader evangelical sympathies of Marsden. Later in the nineteenth century, after other denominations had developed their own missions, the LMS came to depend almost exclusively on Congregationalists for support.

In 1796 the LMS missionaries were designated at the Zion Chapel, London, where public excitement was such that 'multitudes'[7] of well-wishers were turned away at the doors. The congregation inside heard the party described as men 'in the habit of expounding and praying' all 'filled with holy zeal to serve the best interests of the natives in the South Sea Islands' by way of introducing them to 'the principles of useful knowledge, and true religion'. The climax of the service saw four missionaries present themselves for ordination by prayer and the laying on of hands. Apart from exhortations to good works, the missionaries underwent no other preparatory training. As a society, the LMS counted zeal and piety above book learning and a missioner's knowledge of his own religion seldom went beyond what he had picked up listening to other people's sermons, at prayer meetings or in private Bible reading. Some of the later missionaries spent a period attached to a clergyman, especially if they were considered backward, before Bogue opened a seminary for them in 1801. Even then missionary education remained synonymous with Biblical knowledge and referred chiefly 'to the heart'. 'Instead of cherishing the desire of shining in the world by distinguished talents', candidates were instructed to 'aim at subduing every elating thought, and at mortifying the vain propensities of our nature'. [8]

The previous occupations of the four ordained men were respectively schoolmaster, actor, block-maker and printer; and among their colleagues were carpenters, a shoemaker, a hatter, a tailor, a butcher, an ironworker, a shopkeeper and a gentleman's valet. [9] The directors of the LMS claimed that the thirty-six missionaries had all been 'very carefully selected' on the criterion of 'None but men the most select for piety',[10] whose skills were 'in such useful arts and occupations as would make us most acceptable to the heathen in that state of inferior civilization to which they were advanced'. However, several of the vocational skills represented were of no earthly use on a tropical island. Some missionaries were selected because they were such poor preachers that English congregations would not suffer them; others have been depicted as 'illiterate and ruined tradesmen';[11] and a number were included because they alone were left after the scholarly applicants had been diverted to India or the Orient where the work of conversion was thought to demand more sophisticated philosophers.[12] For most of these 'tinkers', acceptance as a missionary meant a rise in social status and opportunities for personal adventure and private Utopia-building based on a corporate certainty that their actions were God's plan and their labours, His glorification. [13]

When they entered the Pacific, the missionaries discovered that Western civilization had preceded them. The South Seas were experiencing a trading boom in spirits and muskets, and its islanders were suffering the ravages of venereal disease and the infliction of white-scum absconders from whalers and traders. After his second voyage there, the phlegmatic Cook had doubts about the effects of the European impact thinking it 'far better for these poor people never to have known our superiority'.[14] Within three decades the missionaries were to achieve many of their aims. The Russian explorer Baron F. G. Bellingshausen, who visited Tahiti in 1820, noted that many natives wore European clothes, tattooing was frowned upon, strong drink and Tahitian dancing and music were banned, and that the weaving of garlands of flowers was forbidden.[15] But had Bellingshausen so wished, he could have purchased a Bible in Tahitian or have invested his surplus cash in the thriving missionary-led coconut-oil trade.

Boats from the *Duff* grounded on a Tahitian beach in March 1797. They landed missionaries at the Friendly Islands and put off the Rev. John Harris and William Pascoe Crook (both of whom were to be closely associated with education in New South Wales) at Santa Christina. But before the *Duff* could weigh anchor Harris was back on board again. He claimed that the islanders' fermented bread-fruit diet gave him chronic indigestion and that he had been physically scared (though not tempted) when several native women, doubtful of his sex, had attempted a nocturnal examination of his person.[16] When eventually the *Duff* returned to England, Haweis proclaimed the day one of thanksgiving and preached a sermon from a letter which Captain Wilson had carried back. 'They have already brought their children for instruction', Haweis read out, 'and our school is opened; many know all their letters, and begin to join them with great docility'.[17] The clergyman also disclosed that a Tahitian magic-maker had sanctioned the missionaries' work with the surprisingly literate comment 'I am too old to learn, but our children will be taught all these wondrous things which we see, and know the speaking book'.

Back in the South Seas the missionaries were encountering serious checks to their progress. Three of them were murdered in the Friendly Islands and the rest driven into the woods by a band of escaped convicts from New South Wales who 'surpassed the heathen in wickedness'.[18] At Tahiti there were quarrels with the natives, missionaries were stripped and their goods stolen, and bitter personal feuds started among them. Two men were excommunicated, one for living openly with a Tahitian, the other for declaring himself an infidel. In 1798 eleven missionaries, four women and four children deserted the main mission to try their fortunes in New South Wales and they were joined by a second party after the Tahitians began fighting among themselves and attributing epidemics of 'the ague, the flux, the venereal disease' to the 'god of England'.[19] A number of these men and women were to return to the islands later and the main Tahitian mission survived to become the centre of LMS activity in the South Pacific.

By the act of leaving their posts, the *Nautilus* men severed any legal connection between themselves and the home Society and, like most colonists, they became dependents of the governor. Nevertheless the Society's directors did not wash their hands of them altogether. They permitted the missionaries to share among themselves the goods which they had salvaged from Tahiti; and they put £200 to their account in the colony, not supposedly for their private benefit, 'but for the purposes of the conversion and civilization of the heathen'.[20] Most of this money was spent on personal bills incurred as the missionaries struggled to establish themselves. Hunter accommodated the party in a house which he was renovating for a school for Johnson and permitted them to fit it out as a chapel.[21] Then he toured the outer settlements to mark out farms for them but few were prepared to try manual labour for a living. When the chaplain required the house for his Hyde Park pupils, the missionaries dispersed themselves voluntarily to the outer settlements where they began itinerant preaching, craft labour and teaching.

As soon as the English directors learned of the Tahitian exodus, they instructed the missionaries to pay special regard to the advice of the chaplains of the Church of England,[22] a direction born of the still sensitive relations between church and dissent at home. It does not surprise then that the colony's governors were unwilling to take the step of inducting the ordained men among them into colonial chaplaincies. However, while they were not prepared to equate the clerical status of the missionaries with that of the government-salaried chaplains, the governors were prepared, 'for want of regular chaplains',[23] to use them for ecclesiastical duties. When so engaged the missionaries were designated acting chaplains and they were paid allowances from colonial funds.

The directors of the LMS had been quick to warn their brethren of the dangers of indiscriminate evangelizing in a penal settlement.

> ... the office of a preacher may be desired by some from a misapprehension of their gifts—or from the idea that it confers distinction, and insures respect—motives of this nature are highly criminal, but yet insensibly sway the deceitfull heart—Our great wisdom and duty is to find out, and occupy that station which providence has qualified us for—[24]

The correspondence to the Port Jackson missionaries also indicated that the directors were not certain whether the governor would permit dissenters to work as schoolmasters in the colony. Under the Act of Uniformity of 1662 all teachers in England were required to conform to the liturgy of the Church of England, subject themselves to the control of the bishops and attend church regularly. By the turn of the eighteenth century, three actions against these restrictions had been tested at law and the point was conceded that a 'court Christian could not have jurisdiction of writing schools, reading schools, dancing schools, and the like'.[25] From 1701 on it was accepted that a Protestant could teach in a non-endowed elementary school without first having to obtain a licence from the bishop.

During these years of restraints on dissenters, a number of underground academies had succeeded in remaining open although their graduates found the universities of Oxford and Cambridge closed to them. Dissenters obtained some relief by the Toleration Act of 1689, provided they were willing to take oaths of 'Allegiance and Supremacy', and, under 13 Anne C7 of 1714, elementary school teachers received exemption from sections of the past conformity legislation. It was not until the passage of 19 Geo III C44 in 1779, however, that dissenters were guaranteed the freedom to maintain their own academies, and even then they were debarred from teaching in endowed schools unless these had been dedicated solely for the children of dissenters or had been founded in or since the reign of William and Mary.

No legal ban existed in England to prevent the missionaries from teaching when the *Nautilus* berthed but there was some uncertainty as to whether British law applied unreservedly in the colony. Marsden once took advantage of this doubt to challenge the right of a missionary to preach on the grounds that the Toleration Act was '*not in force in this country*'.[26] Again, at Marsden's questioning, his assistant chaplain had pleaded before the Parramatta bench that it was improper in Church law for anybody to teach in 'Government Public Schools' without the sanction of the clergy of the Church of England.[27] The bench unanimously rejected the argument. In practice governors did not hesitate to employ dissenters as teachers. While Macquarie is on record for the remark 'I profess to be a member of the Church of England, and wish all to be of the same profession',[28] the acute shortage of teachers, if not any native tolerance, led him to promise the party of LMS missionaries which arrived early in his governorship that 'such of your Members as are qualified to undertake the Education of Youth, will be employed in that capacity, if agreeable to you'.[29]

The welcome given the missionaries at the northern boundary settlements was encouraging at first but with familiarity their congregations fell off. As the summer temperatures rose, morale dropped and 'the Enemy took occasion from these circumstances to suggest the improbability of success'.[30] Rev. William Henry described the New South Welshmen he had fallen among as 'buryed in ignorance and hardened in sin',[31] and his English correspondents read of vices in virtually every known category 'yea, all manner of sin and abominations prevail in this colony—avarice, extortion, pride, theft, blasphemy, drunkenness, sabbath-breaking, fornication, and adultery'. Those of the colonial *élite* whom Henry had supposed would have set an example of church-going, thought it fashionable to stop away and scoffed openly 'at religion and sacred things and treat the holy Scriptures of truth with contempt and ridicule'. When debating religious matters with them, the missionary was obliged 'to lay aside the Bible, as its authority was of no consequence with them' and fall back on philosophical argument for proof of the existence of God.

The knowledge that Bible reading would assure right conduct encouraged the missionaries to persist with plans for education and in time they had classes organized at Kissing Point, Toongabbie and Green Hills. Their first chapel school was at Kissing Point where the congregation of about two dozen was spurred to action by a rumour that the missionaries would desert the district unless more was done for them[32] and on account of 'the prejudice of the people against each other, they not being willing to attend at each other's houses'.[33] By mid-1800, a chapel (30' x 14') with a master's residence attached was erected with building material supplied by the government and from private subscriptions augmented by a £20 loan advanced by Johnson.[34]

On 16 July 1800, eight months later than the organizers had hoped, the Kissing Point chapel and schoolroom was ready for consecration by Johnson and Marsden.

> . . . the Service began at 10 o'clock in the morning by reading the prayers of the Church of England at the end of which was Sung the 97th Hymn the Rev. G. Burders Supplement—Dear Shepherd of &c &c after which the Rev. R. Johnson preached from these words, "And I beseech you Breth. Suffer the word of Exhortation" Heb 13th 22d, there was Sung the 96 Hymn of the Rev. G.B. Supplement, viz. "And will the great Eternal God" &c &c after Service there was three children baptized and the congregation dismissed, Mr. J in his sermon was very faithful to the hearers exhorting them to attend to the concerns of their own Souls to their familys and all around them, in the discourse there was a many very pertinent remarks made & I hope some good done, at least I can say that I found some Searchings of heart, that proved usefull to me in the divine life . . .[35]

The schoolroom at Kissing Point was described as 'very comfortable'[36] especially when compared with the hut the missionaries used at Toongabbie which had 'no floor walls windows or shutters & at this time of the year the hearers tremble with cold, which takes their attention off from the word'. After a visit to catechize the twenty scholars at Kissing Point, Hassall reported that all paid 'good attention to their School, as well as divine Service on Sundays and made good progress in learning so that some of them will soon read well in their Bibles—their Names are all Registered and their attention as well as non-attention took notice of and Rewarded accordingly'.[37] Hassall's concern for the Kissing Point school was recognized officially when King named him its supervisor and directed him to maintain it in good order. This was irrespective of the fact that he was an LMS missionary not a priest of the Church of England.

The Kissing Point master was a man of the missionaries' own choosing, an ex-corporal of the Irish militia named Matthew Hughes, who had the reputation of 'a sincere convert'[38] having joined in prayer meetings with 'Mr. Wesley's people in Ireland'. Hughes had been transported when the men under his command killed a man in a skirmish. The convict was released for teaching by Hunter and kept himself and family alive on a government ration, school fees

and a subsidy of 4d. weekly per child for teaching the children of
pauper parents.[39] Hughes earned himself a conditional pardon under
King[40] and was to teach ten years at Kissing Point before transfer-
ring to a school at Wilberforce.[41]

The missionaries' second chapel school was built for them by the
government at the Green Hills settlement later known as Windsor.
Its master was missionary J. Harris, an ex-cooper by trade who had
served as acting chaplain at Norfolk Island where his activities were
reported on by Major Foveaux.

> Mr. Harris the Missionary is very attentive to the Children. I cannot
> however persuade him to live in the Town, and it is very inconvenient
> for Children to go any distance to a day School and although I believe
> him to be a very good Man he is very unfit for a Minister.[42]

Harris left the island in debt, saved from gaol only when Marsden
discharged his obligations, and, on the chaplain's advice, he pitched
his tent on the banks of the Hawkesbury to be first inside when the
government finished the school building. While he was waiting, the
missionary

> ...rented a house open'd it for divine Service & a day School in which
> Situation I continued near 2 years while Governor King was errecting a
> spacious brick building 100 feet long & 26 feet wide for a place of
> worship & an Orphan School, which I have inhabited several months,
> but the building is not yet finished I preach according to the ability that
> God giveth twice on a Lord's day & catechise the biggest of my children
> after the first part of the Church of England Service is read—[43]

Just before the Green Hills school opened, the editor of *The
Sydney Gazette* spared a paragraph to draw the attention of the public
to its avowed purpose of illuminating 'the infant mind by the
inculcation of moral principles, and the help of such branches of
useful instruction as are absolutely necessary to rescue the rising
generation from the morbid glooms of ignorance'.[44] But there was
not much profit in this high endeavour. Harris reported:

> ... but very few has contributed anything—my Provision is chiefly salt
> Irish pork & sometimes it is very bad & I would be very thankful to you
> to send me a Cheshire cheese—also a few yards of black cloth to make me
> a suit of cloths & 2 or 3 pairs of black stockings & a little Irish linen—

> *PS.* My increase is very small. I preach a free gospel and keep almost a
> free school, I have taught between forty & fifty children within these
> four years & I have not received thirty pounds in the whole—I have
> often sold the proportion of meat I have from the store to support my
> expenses & preserve myself a cloathing agreeable to my Station which

in this country is extremely dear nothing less than a hundred, 200 and 300 pr cent is put upon these articles by the dealers before they come to our hands.[45]

In time more suitable arrangements were made for Harris's upkeep. In addition to his ration, the governor allowed him a small cash allowance from the orphan school fund and for a period he was comfortable and secure in his new brick residence attached to the two-storied building with its cultivated and fenced garden.

The most enterprising of the LMS teachers was Crook, a gentleman's servant early in his career who had moved up the occupational scale to tinworker by the time he joined the *Duff* party.[46] Captain Wilson singled him out as a person 'remarkably serious and steady, always employed in the improvement of his mind',[47] and he recorded something of the thought the missionary had put into his preparations for the Santa Christina landing 'has various kinds of garden-seeds, implements, medicines, etc.; an Encyclopedia, and other useful books'. The captain discerned 'a very good genius' in Crook, one certain to 'contrive many things to benefit the poor creatures he lives with'. Once ashore the solitary missionary set about learning Tahitian to such effect that some natives, astounded by his combination of linguistic fluency and skin whiteness, considered him a god.[48] Later, when Crook's evangelical purposes became better known, the indigines of Santa Christina changed their minds about him and he took a hurried passage on a passing trader.

Returning to England, the missionary achieved popularity as a speaker on South Seas life until the lure of the Pacific saw the recently-married Crook join the party to settle Port Phillip in 1802. When the settlement was prematurely abandoned the Crooks sailed for Sullivan Bay, Van Diemen's Land, where the missionary again taught and preached and where he claimed to have two congregations and seventy-seven children under his care.[49] Then the couple tried mainland New South Wales. Encouraged by Marsden and Hassall, they opened a public school at Parramatta but it happened that the governor had other plans. King wanted Crook to return to Port Dalrymple as storekeeper and acting chaplain, so once again the family set out. This time the vessel carrying them turned back to Port Jackson following a shipboard dispute. During five stormy weeks at sea Crook had identified qualms of conscience about deserting his Parramatta congregation. 'The parents of the children felt their loss', he assured himself. 'The pious people mourned and prayed over it'.[50] Crook was led to interpret his misadventure as a sign from Providence and he gave up thoughts of a Van Diemen's Land sinecure for good.

The entire episode left the family 'no particular favourites'[51] with

King who told Crook he could expect no further encouragement in his school unless he was willing to go south. Even so the governor was not prepared to see the Crook family destitute on the mainland and he accommodated them rent free in a government house rationing them from the stores. This did little to satisfy the missionary who complained that 'convicts just arrived in the colony have a greater encouragement than this'.[52] He wanted an assigned convict and, especially, a salary for he was dependent for his cash income almost entirely 'on teaching prisoners' children only or almost wholly and the higher class of parents will not send theirs to mix'. Disillusioned, the 'little swaddling chap' vented his spite on King referring to him as 'one who governs arbitrarily and capriciously in too many instances'.[53]

The man's considerable teaching abilities soon resolved his problems. In a short time the missionary had three times the enrolments of other masters. 'Everyone', he boasted, 'is desirous for me to instruct their children'.[54] Crook's enrolments climbed to seventy several of whom were fee-paying boarders attracted perhaps by his skilful use of the advertising medium of *The Sydney Gazette*.

NOTICE

Mr Crook has resumed the charge of the Public School kept in Parramatta Church; and wishing to have a few young Gentlemen to Board and Lodge with him, he has taken a House where he can accommodate them.

The Branches of Instruction will be adapted to the Situation for which the Pupil may be designed, who will be taught to read, speak, and write the English Tongue with accuracy and propriety, Book keeping, Geometry, Trigonometry, and Mensuration, practically applied in Navigation, Surveying, Gauging, etc. He will endeavour to store their minds with a general knowledge of Geography, History, and Astronomy, making every part of Education as pleasing as possible.[55]

Success led Crook to abandon his government school in favour of a private academy charging fees of £27 per annum in cash or £30's worth of wheat or pork.[56] After eighteen months the missionary moved his school to Sydney where his wife kept a store and where he ran an after-hours class 'for the good of those adults whose motto is, "Better late than Never"'.[57] This Sydney school was probably the first in New South Wales to attempt the Lancastrian monitorial system of classroom practice.[58] As well as teaching, Crook continued preaching and studying medicine at Sydney Hospital,[59] and, in his spare time, he acquired a knowledge of printing and worked on a Tahitian version of the Gospel of St Luke.

The missionary's move into private enterprise was a sensible precaution for he was to break with the Anglican establishment shortly after joining with John Hosking, master of the female orphan school, and three LMS missionaries to found a church 'on the Congregational or Independent plan'[60] in his Bligh Street school in 1810. Then followed the incident of an unauthorized service in a Hawkesbury public school which saw Crook threatened with deportation from the colony.[61] No doubt Marsden was much relieved when, as colonial agent for the LMS, he found himself in the position to approve the missionary's application to return to the islands. Crook laboured in the South Seas for nearly twenty years before returning to Sydney in 1831 where he re-opened his school and became co-founder of the Australian School Society, the New South Wales version of the British and Foreign School Society.

The *Coromandel* settlers comprized the second group of dissenters and non-conformists active in colonial education before 1810. This was a party of eighteen men and women and twenty children who, chafing at the restrictions of the Toleration Act, emigrated to New South Wales in 1802. Following a short period at Toongabbie, they made permanent homes for themselves on the Hawkesbury flats.[62] Probably the best known was James Mein, the Presbyterian elder and catechist, whose character was aptly summed up by the reference which gained him entry as a free settler to Botany Bay.

> . . . a Man of religious character and unblemished morals, of a quiet and industrious disposition, an affectionate husband and father well affected to the excellent constitution of our country, and by his example likely to prove a blessing to the neighbourhood whence he may settle.[63]

In 1808 a party of *Coromandel* men gathered at the Hawkesbury home of Dr Thomas Arndell where they entered into an agreement to erect a chapel-school at Ebenezer. A contract was let for 3,000 ft of timber at 20s. a 100 ft to be paid for in storage wheat at the rate of 10s. a bushel or live pigs at 9d. or fresh pork at 1s. a lb. The group also accepted a tender for building a stone wall at 8s. a sq. yard.[64] A year later Hassall described their progress:

> For these last Six Months we have endeavoured jointly to dispence the word of life in the district of Portland head which is situated near one of the extramities of the Banks of the River Hawkesbury where the settlers have been very attentive & come forward by subscription to Erect an House for the worship of god and a Schoolroom who with the assistance of a few gentlemen there is nearly £200 subscribed towards defraying the expence of the Building and one of the Setteters' named Owen Cavanough has given 4 acres & 11 Rod off his Farm to—Build the chaple upon its a Most Beauty full and centry cal spot which we have—called Ebenezer Mount—the Institution is named The Portland head Society for the Propagation of Christian Knowledge and the Instruction

of youth—It is under the Management of a Treasurer Secretary and a committee of Severn Landholders—and we hope & trust that you will pray that it began it may be carried on under a divine Blessing and prove of the greatest advantage to the Rising youth of that—Part of the colony as well as the gate & door of heaven to many Precious Souls.[65]

Hassall wrote home for school-books, hymnals and Bibles for the new chapel-school and note of a successful collection appeared subsequently in the *Evangelical Magazine*.[66]

On its completion in 1809, the Portland Head chapel (40' x 20' x 12') stood as one of the colony's most substantial buildings. Stone for its two-foot thick walls was cut with gad and hammer from a nearby outcrop and was carted to the site by bullocks, the framework was of logs adze-trimmed and the roof of stringy bark shingling. Close by was a baker's oven. Many of the settlers would have paid for their children's schooling in wheat, the grain being taken by boat across the river to Arndell's mill to be ground into flour for the teachers and scholars.[67]

The master at Ebenezer was John Youl, an LMS missionary, whose application was agreed to by the committee who accepted his three propositions: a promise to marry; that he would act as minister without payment for one year; and his willingness to grant 'liberty for any good gospel minister, without regard to sect, who might be invited to preach'.[68] Youl was wed in January 1810 and the couple ran a day and boarding school in the church, Jane and the girls sleeping in the attic, John and the boys on the floor below. In 1813 the family sailed for England where Youl was ordained a priest of the Church of England. Later he returned to Van Diemen's Land as government chaplain where he employed a married convict to keep the parish school which received favourable mention in the Bigge *Report* 'the appearance and attainments of the scholars did credit to their teacher, as well as to the attention that had been bestowed upon them by the reverend chaplain himself'.[69]

A number of LMS missionaries who resorted to the Port Jackson staging post attracted unfavourable attention to themselves. These migratory 'gospel venders and bacon curers'[70] peddled articles of trade around the outback, traded in spirits or attempted to live like parasites off the labour of others. Others lived in adultery, consorted with prostitutes or were notorious drunkards. Understandably there was much public cynicism about the genuineness of their religious professions. Bitter faction fights born of feuds in the islands often dominated their private affairs, while the will-sapping charity of the governor and the helpfulness of the Anglican clergy made them vulnerable to charges of an unwillingness to make the sacrifices necessary to establish a permanent colonial church of their own.

But there can be no denying the contribution of these men to colonial education in the initiation, staffing and supervision of schools outside the major settlements. Of the original *Duff* party, at least twelve men were associated with colonial education at one time or another. Both J. Cover, an experienced schoolmaster from Woolwich, and the joiner, W. Henry, taught in colonial schools; and, despite a reputation for being 'rather illiterate than otherwise', the silk-weaver, R. Hassall, dedicated himself to opening them. The tailor and gunner, E. Main, taught in the Airds district and at Minto; J. Cooper, a shoemaker, kept a school at Kissing Point; and another shoemaker, F. Oakes, was a sponsor of the colonial Sunday school movement. W. Crook was seldom without a school as one of his many enterprises; the cooper, J. Harris, taught at Norfolk Island and Windsor; and S. Clode, a gardener, was an early worker among the Aborigines. W. Shelley, a cabinet-maker, managed the Black Native Institution for Macquarie in 1815; while J. Eyre, a block-maker, was one of two missionaries selected by Macquarie to launch his charity school movement in 1810. Another of Macquarie's schoolmasters was W. Smith, a draper, trained in the monitorial system who had taught for a brief spell in New York.[71]

In retrospect the missionary influence on life in New South Wales was less than many had hoped or expected. Instead of converting the convicts and the native heathen, the missionaries concentrated their endeavours on the small communities disposed to receive them. As a group they are best remembered for their activities in fostering schools rather than for their encouragement of the colony's religious life. While no governor chose to laud their religious impact, King went out of his way to commend their achievements in education in a despatch to Hobart. Following his inspection of the missionaries' schools at the outer settlements in 1804, he declared himself confident of 'the progress that learning (and I hope good morals) is making in the younger part of this colony'.[72]

Chapter VIII

CHILD WELFARE
AND COLONIAL ORPHANAGES

> The Establishing a School for Orphans is an
> Act every Parent must acknowledge to be an
> instance of your Humanity & Benevolent
> Feelings, and which after your Demise
> (Which we pray God to keep at a Great
> distance) is likely to remain as long as the
> Island is Inhabited, a Monument to Com-
> memorate, and insure, the Respect and
> Veneration of Posterity to your Name.
>
> Address to
> LIEUTENANT-GOVERNOR P. G. KING
> from seventy-four Norfolk Island Settlers.[1]

En route to Port Jackson, the First Fleet called for fresh provisions at
Teneriffe where the governor's staff was sumptuously entertained by
the Marquis de Branceforte who invited them to make a tour of the
island. The officers were especially impressed by a workshop for the
aged and destitute which worked its inmates at the cottage industries
of sewing and weaving and in the manufacture of ribbons, tapes and
coarse linen. The workshop demonstrated to influential colonists
what a well-organized system of social relief could achieve. Tench
praised its 'excellent regulations'[2] and King, who 'thought it of
infinite service to the common people', recorded in his journal how

> ... every female who is left an orphan, or who is distressed, has only to
> present themselves in order to partake of the humane benevolence of the
> founder. When we were there the number of females was 120, from 7
> years old to 20; and 60 from 20 to 90. The sale of their work maintains
> them, and ye surplus goes to a fund for portioning off those that has been
> there seven years, from ye age of 12, and to provide for those whose age,
> &., may exclude from ye addresses of a suitable husband.[3]

In post-Reformation England provision for destitute children can
be traced back to Edward VI's instruction to Bishop Ridley:

87

... to take out of the streets all the fatherless children and other poor
men's children that were not able to keep them, and to bring them up to
the late dissolved house of the Greyfriars, which they devised to be a
Hospital for them, where they should have meat, drink, and clothes,
lodging and learning and officers to attend upon them.[4]

This ex-Franciscan monastery was re-named Christ's Hospital and
its dormitories soon housed 400 boys and girls who were taught
reading and writing. Those thought to have no aptitude for higher
learning were then apprenticed with a small group remaining behind
for post-elementary studies in the hope of gaining a university place.

By the Poor Law of 1601 parishes were made responsible for
caring for the destitute. This led to forced apprenticeships arranged
by the owners of workhouses or the hiring out of children by private
contractors. What happened to these 'infant and able poor' was
detailed in the Reports of 1775 and 1776.[5] Infants were put out to
nurse at 3s. a week on the parish until such time as they reached
four years of age when they were returned to the workhouses or, if
their labour was worth 6d. a day to a master, they were apprenticed.
Children in the workhouses spent their days picking oakum, teasing
horse-hair and spinning until, 'in rotation as they can be spared from
their work',[6] they were taught to read by the workhouse schoolmaster.

Judging by the salaries at their command, the teaching abilities
of these workhouse masters must have varied considerably. At St
James', Westminister, which boarded 393 children seven years of age
or younger in 1774 (that year 98 of them died), the master was paid
£20 per annum. But at other centres a teacher's labours were
remunerated by a sum as low as 3d. weekly. A workhouse schoolmaster had always to vie with the taskmasters for the children's
time and, in some centres, he competed with production incentives
as well. At Gloucester county workhouse seven year olds were
allowed 1d. in every shilling earned for putting heads on pins. In
practice there was little profit to be had from working child labour
in institutions. At the workhouse of St Martins in the Fields,
Westminster, it was valued at £225 annually compared with the
institution's running cost of £5,016. The money in child labour was
in the factories, mills and mines, whose proprietors seldom provided
formal education. An exception was David Dale at New Lanark in
the 1790s who engaged three full-time teachers and thirteen part-
time assistants to teach over 500 pauper apprentices reading,
writing, music and sewing, after supper.[7] He also ran two full-time
infants' classes for children considered too young to work.

English habits of dealing with the destitute were exported to
Virginia and Massachusetts where poor law legislation had been

enacted in the seventeenth century. At Halifax, Nova Scotia, an orphanage opened in 1752,[8] and a public orphanage was founded at Charleston, South Carolina, in 1790.[9] The colonists of New South Wales found it necessary to experiment with various methods of child care soon after the Farm Cove landing. The first plan Phillip tried allowed an extra adult ration to approved couples willing to board an unwanted child. One who took advantage of his offer was Isabella Rosson, the schoolmistress of 1789.[10]

Boarding out was an inadequate solution in a colony where family life was notoriously unstable. Some believed that marriages contracted in the colony were not legally binding, while others, who had married in anticipation of extra indulgences from the governor, petitioned for a return to their former state when they were disappointed. Many preferred *de facto* liaisons, the muster of 1806 revealing 807 illegitimate births and 1,025 legitimate.[11] A variation on the boarding-out method was tried in 1789 when a boy of three and a girl of four were put under the care of Mrs King at Norfolk Island as 'children of the public'.[12] The boy had lost his mother on the passage out, while the girl's mother was judged of 'so very abandoned a character' that her child was taken from her. Phillip ordered King to cultivate ten acres of land for them, its produce to go to the women prepared to board them and teach them reading, writing and husbandry. As part of his plans for the protection of all the Norfolk Island children, King issued an order prohibiting anyone from leaving the island unless he had made adequate provision for his dependents.[13]

In 1795 King decided to open a small orphanage at Norfolk where 'lost'[14] girls in need of 'a strict hand and eye' could be taught reading and handicrafts. This was no centre for religious teaching like the boarding charity schools of England or a factory where work was undertaken by children for a cash return, rather it attempted the task of teaching the girls uncomplicated, useful skills befitting their futures as working-class mothers. To maintain the orphanage, King relied on port dues, fines, quit rents and voluntary contributions from his officers. However, the sums collected barely kept the inmates 'in scanty clothing'.[15] When King left Norfolk he reminded his successor, Major Foveaux, that 'the future welfare of the Australian Colonies' depended on 'the education and protection of the children' and suggested he extend the orphanage so 'perfecting the foundation which I look upon as hardly begun in the State I left it'.[16]

Foveaux was unable or unwilling to staff the orphanage after some original appointees had been indicted for 'improper conduct'.[17] King did his best to encourage him to overcome reverses by authorizing the re-building of the orphanage at government expense to enable the speedy withdrawal of 'these unfortunate Children from their abandoned Parents'. But Foveaux despaired. In 1801 he replied:

> . . . Having repeatedly considered the miserable situation of the Children at the orphan School for want of proper attendants which cannot be procured here, I beg leave to suggest to your Exy. the benefit that would arise to them could they be sent to Port Jackson and the Money collected on this Island for that Institution be also transmitted and added to your Fund—[18]

It is not known whether any governor took up the major's recommendation before Norfolk Island was evacuated in 1808.

Efforts by King on behalf of destitute children at Norfolk Island had not been duplicated on the mainland although as early as 1796 Johnson had claimed that he could have filled an orphanage from the totally neglected children around Sydney.[19] Marsden too had written of the many children 'totally relinquished and cast upon Government for support and protection';[20] they were, he hypothesized, the offspring of 'itinerant sailors, soldiers, or prisoners' and, less forgivingly, of 'unnatural mothers'. Hunter had planned to establish schools on the Norfolk Island pattern from sums raised from petty licences but a demand by his judge-advocate for one third of any fees collected, frustrated his attempts.[21] The governor became convinced that cash contributions from England would be necessary for any foundation to succeed. However, a few guessed otherwise. Men like Colonial Secretary Collins argued that if anything was to be done at all, it would have to be done by the local administration.[22]

The most common arguments used to justify an orphanage in New South Wales relied for their persuasiveness on the rising generation idea and on the benefits expected to follow from the enforced separation of parent and child. An orphanage was said to be essential as 'the principal hopes are from the rising generation'[23] and because of the desirability of separating 'the greater part of these (at present, innocent) members of the community from their vicious parents'.[24] Other arguments appealed to colonists' patriotism with claims that a disciplined body of colonial orphans promised 'a future source of strength . . . for the defence of His Majesty's dominions'[25] and to their sense of economy by pointing out that the housing of destitute children in institutions would reduce the cost of the boarding out system by at least a third.[26]

The exploitation of young girls in New South Wales was undoubtedly encouraged by the imbalance between the sexes. The kindly Hunter told of the 'most infamous characters'[27] of colonial girls, King found 'much to eradicate'[28] in them, and Mrs Elizabeth

Paterson, wife of the lieutenant-governor, thoroughly approved the notion that 'These children are to be entirely secluded from the other people, and brought up in habits of religion and industry'.[29] Marsden made the additional point that the output of moral females must necessarily improve the habits of their consorts.[30] A colonist was thought unreasonable if he dared query the assertion that the production of 'faithful industrious wives' was better *a priori* than the 'idleness, and uncleaness, and robbery'[31] said to occupy a destitute child's day. The variety and weight of the arguments presented for an orphanage proved overwhelming. Faith in its social efficacy effectively stifled discussion of viable alternatives and it became its own justification. Something of the optimism associated with the project was evident when it became known as the female orphan school or the orphan house rather than the orphan workhouse or the orphan asylum.

Johnson had collected £200 towards the orphanage by early 1800 but he lent the money to the government to pay for the rebuilding of the Sydney Gaol.[32] Plans did not move forward again until King arrived from Norfolk Island to replace Hunter as governor. The change-over of administrations took a protracted five months during which time King took charge of the orphanage's preliminary organization. Hunter also assisted by donating his personal land grant fees to the fund as well as 'a handsome clock';[33] his generosity was the more significant when it is appreciated that the orphanage was virtually his deputy's private charity and that the two men were not on speaking terms much of the time.

By the end of August 1800, King had made a conditional offer to Captain W. Kent for his two-storied brick home which stood in its own gardens near the tank stream and close to King's Wharf. Kent, who was shortly to leave the colony to sail the *Buffalo* to England, accepted an offer of £1,539 for his home 'the best house in all Sydney none excepted',[34] and threw in at no extra charge an orchard worth £300. He was issued with bills at 90 days sight on the Treasury but had to wait two years for his money, receiving payment only after he had reluctantly threatened to repossess the property.[35]

Immediately Kent accepted the bid, King formed a committee to manage the new orphanage's affairs. Members were the two chaplains, Marsden and Johnson, two colonial surgeons, William Balmain and John Harris, the wife of the lieutenant-governor, Mrs Anna King, and Mrs Elizabeth Paterson.[36] All the men were magistrates and, with the exception of the position of treasurer held by Marsden, all posts were honorary. Work for the committee at 'Mrs. King's orphanage' as it was known, included checking enrolments and auditing accounts, and its terms of reference stipulated that members were responsible for the 'Morals and Behaviour'[37] of the girls. The important duty of matrimonial agent was delegated to Mrs King.[38]

Johnson reported at the first committee meeting on 8 September 1800 that he was keeping 304 gallons of brandy in custody for the orphanage and had a credit balance of £315.[39] The following week cash-in-hand had reached £517[40] and Marsden was permitted to call tenders for a second orphanage at Parramatta estimated to cost £2,000. Apparently his listeners were convinced by the chaplain's plea that 958 children, or the entire child population by the latest count, awaited rescuing from 'the future misery to be expected from the horrible examples that they hourly witness from their parents'. Most parents and guardians of the colony's destitute girls, however, refused to see any advantage in handing them over to the committee for a lengthy period of incarceration. They were not tempted by the thought of them learning needlework, spinning, reading, writing, straw-hat manufacturing and singing,[41] when they were worth their keep at home as shepherdesses or house-helps. When the Sydney orphanage, complete with motto *Esto Perpetua*, opened its doors in August 1801, only thirty-one girls were registered.[42] A disappointing total of two hundred and seventeen 'poor objects'[43] were accommodated up to 1821 most of whom, strictly speaking, were not orphans at all but children whose parents were incapable or not interested in caring for them.

The events of the opening day were described by Hassall in a letter to Rev. G. Burder.

> Last Sunday being the time appointed for the opening of the Orphan School by a sermon being preached on the occasion I thought it my duty to attend, accordingly on Sunday morning Mrs. H. & self took a ride to sydney and returned in the evening.
>
> At ten o'clock divine service began by reading the church prayers—the Hymns sung on this ocasion was out of Devine songs for the use of Children—the first was song 3d. Blest be the wisdom &c. &c. the 2d. song 12th. Happy the Child whose &c. &c. After which the Revd. Mr. Marsden preached from that well chosen text Viz. Psal, 27-v-10—When my father and mother forsake me then the Lord will take me up— In his Introduction he defended the sovereignty of God in his dealings towards the children of Israel in the body of his sermon he gave a true description of the Parents of the Children of this Colony 2d. the childrens exposedness to ruin on all hands—concluding all with an exortation to the children advice to the Teachers and encouragement to the society from the exampel of good Nahemiha Urging them to go forward in the work they had engaged against all opersition—Instructing them under their charge in the knowledge of christ whome to know is life eternal—the church was pretty well attended—and I pray that the Lord will crown the whole with his own Blessing—[44]

The sermon over (it was specially written for publication in England), Marsden led the official party on a tour of inspection

> . . . where we was highly delighted with seeing the girls in the greatest order feasting on excilent sort pork and Plumb puddin, and seemed very happy in their new situation—In short the whole is much better then I could have expected & does much credit to those who have the Management of the Institution,—there are thirty one girls Received into the school for learning Clothing Bed & Board—the daly visitors are Mrs. King and Mrs. Patterson the first two Ladies in rank in the Colony which is much to their Honour, may the Lord own the same for the spread of his kingdom, is the prayer of your &c. &c.[45]

After allowing the girls a few days to settle in, Marsden called again to make 'a beginning to instruct them in the principle of christianity, sung a hymn and went to prayer with them'.[46]

'Smart orphan boys' were thought less in need of physical protection than girls or 'vagrant infants'. Although employment opportunities, especially in regard to learning a trade, were limited before Bligh's time, there was often the chance for an adventurous lad to go to sea, an occupation denied convicts and ticket-of-leave men. An advertisement of the day read:

> Wanted for the Ship Elizabeth, three Apprentices from twelve to fifteen years old, to be bound for the Term of Five Years, on same terms as if bound in England; and for a further Encouragement, when ever the Vessel is in Port, they will have the advantage of an Evening School.
> Apply at the Counting House of Campbell and Co. Sydney.[47]

By the 1800s stories were circulating of male orphans living 'in idleness and vice'[48] and the current popularity of the orphanage notion suggested that the best place to accommodate them would be Kent's Sydney house after the girls had been transferred to the new building at Parramatta. Unfortunately this latter project was delayed by lack of funds. As an interim measure King decided to accommodate the boys in the Green Hills school but an inspection of the site revealed that it was too cramped for extensions without involving the unpopular acquisition of private land.[49] When the Parramatta building was completed in 1818, an orphanage for boys opened in the Sydney house. Its declared object was 'To relieve, protect and provide with lodging, clothing, food, and a suitable degree of plain education, and instruction in some mechanical art, poor, unprotected male orphan children'.[50] Inside, thirty destitute boys between seven and ten years were taught the three Rs, shoe-making, tailoring and gardening until such time as they reached fifteen when they were indentured to tradesmen or farmers.

King determined that, for its own protection, his orphanage must become financially independent as soon as possible. He made the committee an initial grant of 13,000 acres of land at Cabramatta, then passed them the deeds of Grose Farm, a 600-acre government property on the outskirts of Sydney.[51] Much of this land was unimproved and the governor had to revert to his Norfolk Island money-raising schemes 'to provide an immediate cash income. King authorized the naval officer to appropriate dues for the orphan school fund from: the entrance and clearance of vessels with articles of sale; charges for the issue of promissory note blanks; forfeits of port bonds; money from the appropriation of quit rents; fines from persons caught selling liquor during divine service; $1\frac{1}{2}$ per cent. turnover on auctioneers' sales; returns from spirit and butchers' licences; fines for shortweight and unstamped scales; penalties for receiving convicts on board ships; fines for employing absconded convicts; and 5 per cent. on wares not of British manufacture carried from ports east of the Cape.[52] A levy of 2s. 6. a ton on coal known as the King's Dues for Orphans was put on all shipments from the Hunter River intended for home consumption. Unregistered boats were forfeit to the orphanage, as were stray pigs, goats, stallions, underweight bread and cocks seized at cock-fights. Free men were fined £5 for the fund if they fouled the tank stream. Finally, the governor granted the trustees a North Shore watering place where 'those merchant vessels that wood and water there, are to pay for permission'.

In addition the orphanage benefited from a number of private donations. It received gifts of barrels of sperm oil from masters of visiting whalers and was mentioned occasionally in colonists' wills. Commodore Baudin, the French cartographer whose fleet called at Port Jackson in 1802, also wanted to help. He wrote to Mrs Anna King:

The Commander in Chief of the French Expedition of Discoveries to Mrs. King, Octr. 1st, 1802.

Madam

On the Eve of my Departure I take the liberty of sending Fifty pounds Sterling of which I beg your Acceptance to be employed for the benefit of the Orphan Institution altho' a Stranger in the Colony. I hope you will not deprive me of the Pleasure which I receive on this Occasion of proving to you—the Estimation in which I hold that and similar Institutions particularly while they are watched over by Persons, who like you, know how to put a Just value on the present utility and future Advantages of them.

I have the Honor to be
Madam—Your very Humble servt.
(Signed)   N. Baudin.[53]

Mrs King's reply thanked him for his generosity 'bestowed in a Manner that does equal Honour to your Philanthropy and Humanity'. The commodore was sufficiently impressed by the colonial charity programme to make a second donation to the proposed orphanage for boys at Green Hills.[54]

Following Hunter's example, King paid his private land grant fees into the orphan fund.[55] He also supplied the orphanage with one sheep a week from the government herds and his men drew a seine regularly in the harbour for its table.[56] When the commissariat was over-supplied in 1805, King sold the surplus and presented the committee with eight breeding cows, eighty ewes and eighteen wethers from the proceeds.[57] King's persistence in seeking income for the orphanage was demonstrated when he urged the secretary of state to remit a £500 fine for attempted manslaughter if the accused lost his appeal in England.[58] In the first instance the governor's arrangements proved adequate enabling the committee to call tenders to cover such items as the orphans' annual consumption of 5,000 lbs of mutton and pork;[59] and, by mid-1806, the orphanage 'ceased having any Provisions or Support from the Crown'.[60]

The most generous of the institutions many private benefactors was Marsden. On 25 January 1805, the chaplain sent King a letter noting that, when he had been appointed treasurer of the orphan fund, the governor

> . . . was pleased to direct me to receive the sum of 5 percent on the receipts of all monies arising to the Fund, as a remuneration for my trouble. At that time the Institution being in its infancy, and the Funds very low, I declined accepting your liberal offer,—Since the accounts have been wound up to the end of last year there is now a very considerable sum in favor of the Fund. Your Excellency has again directed me to receive 5% upon the sum total that the Orphan Fund has received credit for up to the last Settlement for which favor I feel myself much indebted to you. The Institution being founded in Charity, I have no wish to appropriate any part of the money arising to the Fund to my own personal benefit, but shall at all times be happy to render any assistance to the Institution in my power without Fee or reward. At the same time I have to request that your Excellency will allow me to purchase from Government for the Sole benefit of the Orphans Horned Cattle to the amount of the percentage being £190.10.0 I consider this would be a very considerable increasing property, and at some future period yield much supply to the children. Should my proposals not meet your Excellency's approbation, I have then only to request the Committee through the medium of your Excellency to accept the money and appropriate it to the Benefits of the Orphans in any other way their wisdom may point out.[61]

King sought the committee's advice on Marsden's letter and its members recommended that he take up the chaplain's 'humane offer'.[62] They were careful though to record in the minutes that the percentage they allowed their treasurer was 'very inadequate to the responsibility attached thereto'. By then Marsden's percentage stood at £255. 14s. 6d. and King directed the commissary to supply the orphanage with nine cows and two ewes in liquidation.[63]

Marsden's refusal to draw his treasurer's percentage had cost him over £1,000 by 1821[64] and he was out of pocket to the tune of his turnpike fees and horse and chaise expenses on the road between Parramatta and Sydney. Some of the obvious and justifiable esteem in which the chaplain was held in church quarters in England can be attributed to knowledge there of his generosity towards this 'foundation of religion and morality'.[65] To the clergy at home it was undeniably 'a great work which will go on till the Time of the Millenium'.[66] However, it must be admitted that some clergy were under the impression that the orphanage at New South Wales housed 'about 400 in number between the ages of 5 & 16'[67] instead of the thirty odd it actually accommodated.

The income of the orphan school fund and the gaol fund which together comprised the colonial revenue, was collected from separate lists by the naval officer, J. Harris, who was also a member of the orphan school committee. For his trouble Harris received 10 per cent. of the gross receipts.[68] His clerk assessor was David Dickenson Mann, an ex-convict and one-time schoolmaster, who received 5s. a day for attending to the committee's business plus $2\frac{1}{2}$ per cent. of the gross collected.[69] This income was additional to his cut in helping collect the colonial revenue. In 1810 Macquarie re-named the gaol fund, the colonial police fund. He also directed that the separate list of duties be abolished and the money be divided between the two funds on a percentage basis, 75 per cent. for the colonial police fund, 25 per cent. to the orphan school fund.[70] In 1817 the orphan fund's share of the colonial revenue was cut back to one-eighth.[71]

Whitehall raised no objections to reimbursing Kent for his house and had cheerfully approved the idea of an orphanage after the event. They also agreed in advance to the commissariat's profits for one year being spent on it. However, King was instructed to confine his attention strictly to destitute children.[72] As soon as he received the direction, King convened the committee and ordered a check on each child's circumstances. Any parent the committee thought could afford to do so, was asked to pay an upkeep fee.[73] The willingness of the British authorities to sponsor this expensive charity owed much to the fact that money spent on it was raised within the colony.

Later, when British costs and the local revenue rose sharply, the home treasury took a more sophisticated view arguing that the colonial revenue ought properly to be applied to reduce British expenses. [74]

The first matron of the orphanage was Mrs Elizabeth Hume, [75] a clergyman's daughter and mother of Hamilton who was to pioneer the overland route from Sydney to Port Phillip in 1824-5. With her two assistants, Mrs Hume presided over a staff of eight convicts and ex-convicts. A year later she resigned her £40 per annum post because of family worries and was succeeded by Mary Robinson and next by the Robsons. Mr and Mrs Stroud succeeded them in May 1803. [76] By then the orphan establishment comprised a matron, cook, housemaid, porter, servant, and three teachers on an allowance of six guineas a year each. One of the teachers could not write, she receipted her pay checks 'X'. [77]

The many staff changes undertaken in the search for men and women capable of managing an orphanage typically ended in failure. The worst appointment was the man Bligh nominated after the Strouds had left. His habit was to preach on Sundays and take 'unwarrantable liberties with the Girls on Mondays, for which he is now ordered 200 lashes to stand in the Pillory 3 times, and to hard Labour to Newcastle'. [78] In 1807 Mr and Mrs Marchant took over but Mr Marchant was murdered and the widow stood down in favour of Mr and Mrs H. Perfect who had left a private school to try out for the post. [79] In 1809 the keys were handed to Mr and Mrs J. Hosking recruited for the job by Marsden in England.

Before the arrival of the Hoskings, a delay in making the first appointment cost the committee the chance of employing Rev. J. Cover who returned to England in exasperation. [80] Then the committee offered the post to Crook who declined it on grounds that it was inconsistent with his 'character, comfort or usefulness'. [81] The missionary admitted later that the real reason for his rejection had been the pervading influence of depravity and vice. 'It Seemed impossible as matters then were', he confessed, 'to rectify the dreadful abuses of that institution'. [82] In one attempt to protect the institution's good name, the three magistrate members of the orphan school committee thought it necessary to sentence a man to a flogging.

> An investigation yesterday se'nnight took place at the Orphan House before the Rev. Mr. MARSDEN, THOMAS JAMISON and JOHN HARRIS Esqrs. relative to a scandalous liberty taken with the character & reputation of one of the Orphans, by H. Simpson, who was brought forward and accused on evidence; he admitted that he had, without intention to prejudice used the words attributed to him, which when spoken he supposed could not be credited, as the aspersion was in itself

no less false than ridiculous. By acknowledging the offence though contrition were to be presumed yet example was unfortunately necessary to the prevention of future scandalous and unfeeling attacks of the same kind. Upon the latter consideration he was sentenced 100 lashes, but upon the former, only half that punishment was inflicted; and doubtless every friend to virtue, truth, justice, and humanity will thoroughly accord in the hope that a single example will be sufficient to shield the objects of this benevolent Institution from wanton and uncharitable slander.[83]

After King left the colony Bligh noted 'very improper persons'[84] about the orphanage and two committee men, Harris and Jamison, resigned in protest at conditions there. Bligh then appealed to the secretary of state for competent staff to manage it.[85] When the Hoskings took charge they found the buildings in bad repair and some colonists were depicting it as no better than 'a bawdy house'.[86] Crook alleged:

> . . . the far greater part of the female orphans when they left the school turning out prostitutes and many there is just ground to conclude were little better while in the School. Indeed it is scarcely purged to this day. Mr. and Mrs. Hosking had no expectations of doing good till they had sent out all the elder girls which they have now pretty well done, and the greater part of these turned out as we expected.[87]

Under the Hoskings the institution's administration improved rapidly. Marsden spoke highly of them and of their convict servant girl, Elizabeth Wynne, testifying that they gave the committee 'full satisfaction'[88] from the beginning. Towards the end of Macquarie's governorship efforts by Hosking to organize a separate Methodist Church alienated him from the Church of England establishment; as well he had become unhappy about implementing the Anglican monitorial teaching system in the orphanage when his private preference was for the British and Foreign version. These conflicts probably influenced the family in their decision to return to England in 1819.

Despite their lavish endowments, the committee men found their income barely covered costs and they began to sell spirits on the open market to make ends meet. Expenses were heavy and Bligh's estimate of £1,500 annually to keep the orphanage 'in proper decorum and order'[89] for fifty children proved remarkably accurate. Between 1811 and 1818 running costs alone were just on £10,000;[90] this was exclusive of money spent on building and farm upkeep. Such expenses could have prevented more money being spent on public day schools which received only 10 per cent of the income set aside for education before 1820. A taste of the cost of orphanages apparently curbed enthusiasm for similar ventures. Certainly they came to be held in less regard in England where Collins's attempt to rebuild 'a shell of a building called the orphan school—a shelter alternatively for men and cattle'[91] in Van Diemen's Land in 1807 was disallowed on a technicality in his application.[92]

In the face of much public criticism the Sydney orphanage retained a few fervent supporters. Its revenue collector, Mann, claimed that the home put many girls in the way of 'virtue and industry';[93] and when the committee undertook a formal inspection in 1803, its members discerned 'considerable Improvements both in their Morals and Education, considering the Situations from whence they have been taken'.[94] Bligh, a less partisan observer perhaps, asserted that some inmates had been taken as servants 'by the most respectable people'[95] and were 'very well qualified before they left the school, to read and write, as well as to do all work as sempstresses'. Between 1801 and August 1806, six girls were married from the orphanage and another eleven were apprenticed to the wives of officers;[96] and some children of promise had their fees paid at Crook's private academy from the orphanage's funds.[97]

A measure of the effectiveness of the orphanage is found in its individual success stories. Mary Peat, an inmate who later taught in the orphanage school, was discharged to marry the man King had nominated for public baker at Castlehill in 1803. Answering a plea from the governor to bestow 'a little Portion on the Bride from the Funds as may serve to convince the Children, that it is equally the Committee's desire to see them advantageously placed in Life, as well as to protect them in their Youth',[98] the committee made her a settling gift of £10 in property. Two other orphanage girls, Susannah Humphries and Charity Evans, were teachers at the institution before the matron gave them away. Susannah married the Parramatta identity N. Payten and Charity married T. E. Nott, master of a private commercial school in Sydney.[99]

Although the orphanage was better run internally under the Hoskings, its business affairs were less adequately managed. The new orphanage at Parramatta took five years to build and a serious drought depleted its herds which had been mismanaged by their ex-gunsmith overseer. The aims of the institution were attacked in public by those who wanted it run like 'an House of Industry . . . in order that they may be prepared for Farmers' wives' not as a 'Boarding School for young Ladies who have some Prospects in Life'.[100] The committee method of part-time administrators proved a failure. Men were appointed with no direct interest in the institution who aroused themselves to vote only when they wished to carry some partisan motion. On 1 January 1824, the committee was disbanded by Brisbane who replaced it with nominees of his own headed by the colonial secretary.[101] Two years later the orphanage became the property of the Church of England and its estates were sold to meet the debts of the ailing Church and School Lands Corporation. By then little remained of the institutional credo of 1800, and a new social panacea, the Female School of Industry under the patronage of Mrs Darling, had replaced it as the colony's most fashionable charity.

Chapter IX

EDUCATING THE ABORIGINE

"GOVERNOR,—that will make good
Settler—that's my Pickaninny!"

The Sydney Gazette, 4 January 1817

Early colonial opinion of the extent to which the Aborigine could benefit from formal education was an amalgam of fact, fiction and prejudice. British readers who accepted the arguments of Rousseau's *Social Contract* cast the New Hollander in the mould of a noble savage, a kind of neo-classical man. But others perceived them through Dampier's eyes as 'the miserablest People in the World', members of a race destined for inferiority by Biblical prophecy and representing the lowest link in nature's chain 'at the very zero of civilization, constituting in a measure the connecting link between man and the monkey tribe?'[1] Cook was one of very few to attempt an objective assessment. He appreciated the simplicity of their material wants, their reserves of courage and survival skills in a hostile environment.[2] Their comparative lack of numbers was also noted, a factor taken into account when Botany Bay was chosen for a penal colony.

Officially Phillip was committed to a policy of conciliation towards the Aborigines although he needed no urging to protect 'this innocent, destitute, and unoffending Race'[3] characteristically attributing hostility on their part to acts of provocation by Europeans. But in 1790 his attitude towards the 'children of ignorance'[4] changed: the governor was speared accidentally by an over-anxious native at a ceremonial whale feast and his gamekeeper was discovered mortally wounded. In retaliation, Phillip despatched a party to capture several males of the offending tribe who were to be shot and their heads returned to the settlement in bags presumably for public display. Fortunately for them, the dark people had slipped away by the time the avengers arrived on the scene.[5]

Efforts to win over Aborigines were a conspicuous failure and a policy of capture was instituted in an attempt to get to know them better. The famous Bennilong was secured in 1789 and taken to England with Phillip when the governor returned home. On his return to New South Wales, Bennilong demanded that his relatives 'love each other'[6] and he threatened that he would 'no longer suffer them to fight and cut each other's throats'. The Aborigine asked only that they be 'somewhat more cleanly in their persons, and less coarse in their manners' when they gathered about him. By then he had been sufficiently assimilated to English customs to want to fight his tribal enemies with his fists rather than by club and spear. But the social reformer could not carry even his wife with him. She discarded his gift of a rose-coloured petticoat and gipsy bonnet and abandoned him for a less civilized lover. Instead of 'making himself useful, or showing the least gratitude for the numberless favours that he had received',[7] the frustrated Aborigine involved himself in fights in the township and became 'so fond of drinking that he lost no opportunity of being intoxicated'. The failure of Bennilong's attempt to turn himself into an English gentleman provided further support for those colonists who were arguing that the Aborigines of New South Wales were an innately inferior people.

The first Aborigine captured was Arabanoo who died shortly afterwards from smallpox 'to the infinite regret of everyone who had witnessed how little of the savage was found in his manner, and how quickly he was substituting in its place a docile, affable, and truly amiable deportment'.[8] The same epidemic left a boy, Nanbaree, and a fourteen year old girl, Abaroo, with no parents. Both were eagerly adopted by white foster fathers, Abaroo going to Johnson and Nanbaree to Surgeon-General John White who had him christened Andrew Sneap Hammond Douglass White.[9] Abaroo never settled with the Johnsons. After she had been with her adopted parents for about eighteen months, she 'was so desirous of going away that it was consented to'.[10] The following day Abaroo was seen naked in a canoe but the observer noticed that she had put on a petticoat when the chaplain appeared.

Johnson was disheartened at the outcome of his educational experiment especially since the results of the first year were promising.

> Have taken some pains with Abaroo (about 15 years old) to instruct her in reading, & have no reason to complain of her improvement. She can likewise begin to speak a little English & is useful in several things about our little Hutt. Have taught her the Lord's Prayer etc., and as she comes better to understand will endeavour to instruct her respecting a Supreme Being, etc.[11]

In her time with the Johnsons the girl failed to outgrow her tribal fears and once fell into convulsions on sighting a shooting star. But then the whites about her were not liberated from superstition either: some testified that in her hysterical state she had alluded to the coming wreck of the *Sirius* at Norfolk Island.[12]

Adoption by Europeans did not usually alienate Aboriginal children from their own tribes although one seven-year-old girl from Broken Bay taken into Government House in Hunter's time was found speared to death.[13] Generally these children moved freely between foster home and tribe seeking out their European families again after receiving a beating or two or because of hunger in the camp. For all this, ties between child and tribe remained strong. On one occasion a scuffle between Aborigines and whites saw Phillip organize a party 'to make a severe example of them'.[14] However, his plans were frustrated by young Nanbaree who

> . . . true to his countrymen, on seeing the soldiers form on the parade, ran into the woods, and stripping himself, that he might not be known, joined the natives, and put them on their guard; after which he returned, and seeing the governor go past with some officers, whilst he was hid in a bush, he afterwards shewed himself to an officer's servant, and asked where the governor and the soldiers were going, and being told, he laughed, and said they were too late, for the natives were all gone.

While the tribe seldom rejected their half-civilized members, the antipodal example occasionally applied as in the civilizing of young James Bath related in *The Sydney Gazette* of 2 December 1804:

> On Wednesday a native youth died at Sydney of a dysentery, who was the first of the savage inhabitants of this colony introduced to civil society. When an infant he was rescued from barbarism by the event of his parents' death, both being shot while they were engaged in plundering and laying waste the then infant settlement at Toongabbee. When the pillagers were driven off the infant was found, and compassionately adopted as a foundling by George Bath, a prisoner. The little creature then received the name of *James Bath*.

By way of becoming assimilated James passed through three more foster homes during which time he became isolated from his own people to the extent of testifying to

> . . . a rooted and unconquerable aversion to all of his own colour—also esteeming the term *Native* as the most illiberal and severe reproach that could possibly be uttered . . . with his early alienation from his sooty kindred he seemed to have undergone a total change of disposition from that which forms their characteristic, as he was docile, grateful, and even affable; he took much pride in cleanliness of dress, spoke none but our language, and as he approached his latter end gave undoubted proofs of Christian piety, fervently repeating the Lord's Prayer shortly before his dissolution.

One way or another the certain outcome of the adoption of Aborigine children was the disillusionment of the foster parents. Colonists who anticipated that Aborigines brought up among white people would be 'little disposed to relish the life of their parents', discovered that they invariably quit 'their comfortable abodes' to return to their 'savage mode of living'.[15] Some Europeans lost all hope of civilizing them while others like Johnson continued to believe that these

> . . . ignorant & benighted heathen, will be capable of receiving instruction, but this must be a work of time & much Labour. It wd be advisable & is much to be wished that some suitable Missionary, (two wd be better) was sent out for this purpose.[16]

Marsden held a similar opinion. Like Johnson his experiment in Aboriginal upbringing had begun well.

> . . . I have also a little native boy who takes up part of my attention— He is about six years old—and now begins to read English and wait at table, and hope at some future period he may be a useful member of society. He has no inclination to go among the natives, and has quite forgot their manners.[17]

The chaplain hired a tutor for the boy, but the ingratiate was to abscond at Rio when travelling with the Marsdens to England. The lad was returned to the colony by a friend of Marsden's but died soon afterwards, exhibiting 'Christian faith and penitence'[18] in the Sydney Hospital.

Marsden, who was attached to the theory that industrious work habits must precede the gospel if evangelism in the Pacific was to succeed, considered that election was still further away for the Aboriginal race. His beliefs were based on his first-hand experiences with the two Aboriginal boys he had taken into his home.

> I have found something very peculiar in their constitutions and affections. I think it is hardly possible to attach them to our Habits, Customs and Friendships. I found that to be the case with two that I attempted to civilize and my predecessor the Rev. Richard Johnson found the same want of attachment in two native girls that he took much pains with. One of my boys was taken from his mother's breast & brought up with my children for 12 years—but he still retained his instinctive taste for native food—and he wanted that attachment for me and my family that we had just reason to expect and he always seemed to want that fine feeling of affection which is the bond of social life.[19]

Other colonists shared his pessimism. On the occasion of the burial of Nanbaree in the Kissing Point garden of the Aboriginophile brewer, James Squire, the representative of *The Sydney Gazette* remarked that their ancestral habits were too 'indelibly engendered ever to be eradicated by human effort, however strained in its benevolent design'.[20]

Religious beliefs were often of crucial importance in conditioning European attitudes on the question of the educability of the Aborigine. When Noah cursed Ham, his curse passed down to all the dark races, and to some evangelicals the very thought that a fallen race unredeemed by salvation could possess intrinsic qualities appeared ridiculous. Belief in the moral debasement of the Aborigine was perhaps most completely expressed by J. Dredge, a one-time assistant protector of the race.

> In the licentiousness of their lives they are as the men of Sodom, sinners exceedingly. And the prevalence of those diseases which, amongst men of every nation, constitute the established retribution awarded by the Creator as the just punishment of such abominations—whilst they exhibit the penalty, conclusively establish the existence of the crimes of which they are the legitimate fruits.[21]

Although the English directors of the LMS had instructed their missionaries to convert as many of the native heathen as they had time to attend to,[22] their men in the colony had troubles enough in establishing a mission among nominal Protestants. Most missionaries who had not already accepted that the Aborigine was incapable of instruction declared that the directions from England set them an 'almost impossible task'.[23] Two exceptions were Samuel Clode,[24] unhappily murdered in 1799, and William Shelley, a member of the original *Duff* party who had worked in the Tongan mission. Shelley also acted as a trading agent for Sydney commercial interests and, when he failed to negotiate a more ambitious venture on behalf of his mission, he returned to Sydney to keep a general store in York Street. Back in the islands again in 1813, the missionary narrowly escaped death when his ship was seized by Raiatean pearl divers but he succeeded in recovering her and in sailing the vessel to Port Jackson. The following year the family settled at Parramatta where Shelley conducted Congregational services and began mission work among the Aborigines.[25]

Shelley's attitude towards the Aborigines stemmed largely from his experiences at Parramatta. As he explained to the LMS:

> I have several children for some time and find them remarkably teachable. They have a peculiar aptness in learning the English language and pronounce it with much propriety. From the rambling Naked State of these poor Natives they have generally been supposed as incapable of improvement but I am persuaded that under the blessing of God they are as capable of instruction as any other untutored Savages. It is my

intention should the Lord spare me to learn their language, I have made a beginning & find I shall have a considerable difficulty in attaining it. There appears scarce the least similarity between it and the language of any of the Islanders of the South that I am acquainted with. It is very remarkable that tho' this Colony has been settled near thirty years no one attempted the study of the language of the Natives.[26]

Aboriginal children had to wait for Macquarie to become governor before they were thought fit recipients for the government sponsored schooling of the day. In Macquarie's opinion the Aborigine, though rude and uncivilized, could be transformed into a labourer or semi-skilled worker given 'the fostering Hand of Time, gentle Means, and Conciliatory Manners'.[27] Some evidence supported him for in Hunter's day Aborigines had laboured in the fields with sufficient persistence to earn a ration from the stores,[28] while others found regular employment in the sealing gangs working Bass Strait. Following an exceptionally violent bout of raids by Aborigines on the Hawkesbury harvest in 1814, Macquarie determined to back a plan which Shelley had drawn up to civilize the Aboriginal race through their children. The scheme envisaged

> . . . a Public Establishment Containing one Set of Apartments for boys, and another Separate Set for Girls; let them be taught reading, writing, or religious education, the Boys, manual labour, agriculture, mechanic arts, etc., the Girls, sewing knitting, spinning, or such useful employments as are suitable for them; let them be married at a Suitable age, and Settled with steady religious Persons over them from the very beginning to see that they Continued their employment, so as to be able to support their families, and who had Skill sufficient to encourage and Stimulate them by proper Motives to exertion.[29]

With their training complete, the young folk were to be set up on plots of land with a cow, farming implements and seeds to found a breed of black yeomen.

At Macquarie's insistence, Shelley costed the proposal for a school to accommodate twelve children. Staffing was estimated at £132 per annum, rent at £30, and clothing, coals, candles and books at £85. The estimate for the weekly ration per child was

		s.	d.
To 3½ lbs. Meat @ 7d.		2.	0½
" 2 lbs. Rice		0.	6
" 10 lbs. Corn flour		1.	8
" 2 lbs. Wheat "		0.	8
" ½ lb. Sugar		0.	3
" ¼ lb. Soap		0.	2
" Salt and Pepper		0.	2
		5.	5½[30]

Although quarterly costs fluctuated depending on enrolments, Shelley's budgeting proved realistic, annual costs generally falling a little below his provisional estimates.[31]

When he presented his plan, Shelley was careful to discredit the widely-held belief that the Aborigines were incapable of civilization. He argued that because 'human nature is the same in every Clime', then differences between Aborigines and Europeans were superficial, the result of differences 'of manners and Customs and variety of Circumstances'.[32] Shelley's optimistic argument carefully avoided the fundamentalist corollary that it was precisely because human nature was universally the same, that Aborigines were as besmirched with original sin as their white-skinned brothers. Instead he argued that attempts to civilize them had failed to date not on account of racial inferiority or any inherent sinfulness but because there was no way in which they could retain their independence in Western society. Macquarie accepted Shelley's position and, in a Government and General Order of 10 December 1814, he notified the public that his administration recognized a special responsibility for Aboriginal welfare.

> . . . when it is considered that the *British Settlement* in this Country, though necessarily excluding the Natives from many of the natural Advantages they had previously derived from the animal and other Productions of this Part of the Territory, has never met with any serious or determined Hostility from them, but rather a Disposition to submit peaceably to such Establishments as were necessarily made on the Part of the *British Government* on the Formation of this Settlement.

> With a View, therefore, to effect the *Civilization of the Aborigines of New South Wales*, and to render their Habits more domesticated and industrious, *His Excellency* the *Governor*, as well from Motives of Humanity as of that Policy which affords a reasonable Hope of producing such an Improvement in their Condition as may eventually contribute to render them not only more happy in themselves, but also in some Degree useful to the Community, has determined to institute a *School* for the *Education* of the *Native Children* of both *Sexes*, and to assign a *Portion of Land* for the *Occupancy* and *Cultivation* of Adult *Natives*, under such *Rules* and *Regulations* as appear to *Him* likely to answer the desired *objects*.[33]

At the time Macquarie informed Secretary of State Bathurst of his intentions, he promised to fund the institution for two years from the colonial revenue and, anticipating his approval, he went on to open the school on 'the Auspicious Anniversary of Her Gracious Majesty's Birth Day',[34] 18 January 1815, with five children all 'perfectly happy and reconciled to their new Mode of Life'. These children and most of their successors were recruited from their semi-intoxicated fathers at a government-sponsored feast day for which the commissariat supplied

1 Fat Bullock 500 lb. wt.
200 lb. Bread
100 lb. Potatoes
 20 lb. Sugar
100 Lemons
 10 gals. Rum
Dinner to be ready at 12, o'clock . . . grog—Tub & Tin mugs.

L.M.[35]

The institution was managed by a committee comprizing Messrs Campbell, D'Arcy Wentworth, Redfern and Macarthur, and Revs Cowper, Fulton and Hassall; Shelley was named superintendent and Lieutenant-Governor G. Molle, resident. A notable omission was Marsden. According to testimony taken at the Bigge enquiry, the senior chaplain excluded because

. . . the Gov[r]. consulting Mr. Marsden on the Hope of civilising the native Blacks, Mr. M. gave the Gov[r]. Little hopes of Success, and prevented him from soliciting his assistance in the formation of the Society. Mr. Marsden never showed any sympton of good will towards it. Has never attended the School nor the meeting of the natives. His conduct towards the New Zealanders is a striking Contrast to his Indifference towards the Native Blacks.[36]

However, Marsden has left a different version of the events:

Previous to the establishment of the Native Institution in the year 1814 General Macquarie did me the honor to ask my opinion relative to the civilization of the aborigines of New South Wales, which I readily gave him at that time, observing that there appeared to me to be one great difficulty in the way as far as I was able to form a judgement of their Character—which was, that the Native Inhabitants seemed to want that fine feeling of affection and attachment which are the bonds of Social life—I made this observation to General Macquarie not with a view to discourage any attempt that he had a desire to make to promote their civilization—I wished the experiment to be made, and during our conversation, recommended a Farm near Kissing Point as a proper situation to make a trial . . . During our conversation I also informed General Macquarie that I was authorised by the C.M. Society to assist any plan with pecuniary aid that was likely to benefit the aborigines of this Colony —From that period to the present time General Macquarie never mentioned the subject to me, and therefore no demand was ever made upon the Society funds.[37]

Marsden's exclusion was an outcome of the bitter personal feud between himself and the governor. At the seat of their unconcealed animosities were diametrically opposed concepts of the colony's purpose nowhere more evident than in Macquarie's policies favouring emancipists' rights and Marsden's sympathies for the cause of the exclusives. Macquarie argued that had he included Marsden on the committee, Shelley's efforts would have been impeded. There was the point, too, that the missionary followed the plan of the British and Foreign School Society which allowed Bible reading and Sunday school attendances but no catechetical instruction and, should the committee have accepted an Anglican Society grant, then Shelley would have been required to teach the catechism of the Church of England to meet their conditions or else resign. Marsden's resentment at his exclusion effectively precluded any co-operation between himself and the institution. As he informed Bigge:

> I certainly thought it Singular that two Dissenters should be appointed, one a Member of the Committee and the other Superintendent of the Institution, and two of the Assistant Chaplains at a distance, while the Senior Chaplain was never mentioned tho' the Institution was close to his Church. This was a matter of surprize not only to myself but the Colony. The Governor could not seriously expect me either to attend the School or the Meeting of the Natives when His Excellency had shewn such a marked inattention to my public situation as Senior Chaplain and Minister of Parramatta without any offence of mine. The Governor asked me my opinion of the Natives. I gave it him candidly without intending to offend and the opinion I then gave I have seen no reason to alter yet I should have been most happy to have seen the native Inhabitants improve in civilization and morals & would willingly have contributed my assistance towards their improvement had I been called upon by the Governor to take a part in the work. I could not intrude myself into a public Institution without authority or invitation without running the risk of giving offence to my Superiors and subjecting myself to public animadversions.[38]

From its inception the school had difficulty holding its Aboriginal scholars. Although Macquarie had written to Bathurst that the children were perfectly happy in their new surroundings, they did not take readily to confinement.[39] After nearly six months as superintendent, Shelley admitted to a friend that Aboriginal parents were 'remarkably backward to give up their children',[40] and once they had enrolled them, despite the strictest promises to the contrary, they invariably returned in attempts to decoy them away again. In 1816 Macquarie tapped a fresh source of enrolments when he sent

> ... two fine Boys named *Nalour* and *Dooro*— and two girls named *Mybah* and *Betty*—Black Natives—all being about 8 years of age, lately taken Prisoners along with the Hostile Native Tribes, to the School or Native

Institution some time since established at Parramatta for the civilization of the Aborigines of this Country; these 4 Children having themselves expressed a wish to go to the Institution and to remain in it.—They were accordingly sent up thither this morning in the Passage Boat in charge of one of the Sydney Constables.[41]

Of thirty-seven admitted, ten had died, absconded or been removed by their own kin by the end of 1820.[42] Among the absconders were Nalour and Dooro.

Shelley died in July 1815, and it was not until Mrs Shelley and her daughter established themselves that enrolments rose again. At the end of the quarter to 30 June 1815 only five children were in full attendance; however, by 31 December 1818 there were fourteen, reaching a total of twenty-seven on 28 December 1820.[43] Generally Aboriginal parents remained unconvinced of the utility of the institution despite the fact that their children were paraded in front of them regularly to read their lessons and show specimens of written work. The problem of retention was well illustrated by the fate of the school's open paling fence. Originally it had been devised to enable Aboriginal parents to peer in to see how well their children were being looked after but the same openings provided a route to freedom. It was dismantled and replaced by an escape-proof wall.[44]

The academic apogee of the institution was reached in 1019 when twenty Aboriginal children competed in the Anniversary School Examination at Parramatta with some one hundred Europeans where, to the chagrin of some, 'a black girl of fourteen years of age, between three and four years in the school, bore away the chief prize'.[45] By then Macquarie considered that the institution had 'fully answered the purpose for which it was established'[46] and that it had 'proved' that Aboriginal children were 'susceptible of being completely civilized'. Even the governor's severest critic, Commissioner Bigge, was to comment in his report that the school was a very creditable achievement.[47] Bigge recorded that thirty-seven boys and twenty-seven girls had been admitted as inmates since its inception (careless counting for the combined total was thirty-seven), and that two girls had been hired out as servants to 'respectable inhabitants in the country'. However, the Commissioner concluded on the cautious note that it remained to be seen 'whether the habits they acquire in the schools are permanent'.

The turning point in the history of the institution came with Macquarie's departure in 1822 and Mrs Shelley's retirement that year. Despite enthusiastic praise from Macquarie in London that the progress of the children was 'a subject of astonishment to every one, who has ever visited the Institution',[48] its secretary was admitting privately to the Bishop of London that the school was 'not in a flourishing state'.[49] In 1838 Mrs Shelley was to voice her disillusionment with the entire project:

> Several of the girls had married black men, but instead of having the effect intended, of reclaiming them, they eventually followed their husbands into the bush, after having given away and destroyed all the supplies with which they had been furnished by the government.
>
> Since that period, some of them have occasionally visited me, and I found they had relapsed into all the bad habits of the untaught natives. A few of the boys went to sea, but I have not heard what has become of them. Most of the girls have turned out very bad, but there is one exception in a half-caste girl, who was married to a white man, and was very industrious, taking in needlework, etc. I have not, however, heard of her for two years.
>
> I have frequently conversed with them since, on religious subjects, but they turned them into laughter, and said they had forgotten all about it.[50]

The restricted and piecemeal development of Shelley's institution was apparent to the Church of England chaplain Rev. W. Cartwright who urged a comprehensive scheme of his own on the government. The chaplain was confident that 'Buried as is the intellect of these Savages in Augean filth, we may yet find Gems of the first Magnitude and brilliance',[51] and he proposed the establishment of a settlement in an isolated part of the Cowpastures to be named Macquarie City where a community programme would be undertaken with the assistance of natives previously trained by the Shelleys. Macquarie determined to reserve 10,000 acres of land for the project[52] but plans were shelved when he returned to England.

On Macquarie's departure the institution fell under the control of Marsden who cleansed it of dissenters and fostered links with the Church Missionary Society. After Mrs Shelley resigned it was moved from Parramatta to Blacktown where the children were put in the care of a missionary, Mr Clark, whom the chaplain had diverted from New Zealand.

> I have the pleasure to inform you that Mr. and Mrs. Clark arrived here a few months ago—They are very promising young people—I have deemed it prudent for the present to detain them in the Colony, until things in N. Zealand are a little more settled—when remonstrating with Mr. Kendall on the Impropriety of his Conduct in bartering Muskets with the natives, he attempted to justify the measure by informing me that Society was going to send out to Shunghee a Gun Smith named Mr. Clark—I told him Mr. Clark would not be allowed to come to N.Zealand upon those Terms, for I should retain him in the Colony— I am persuaded it will be better for the present to keep him here until I write to N.Zealand, and inform Mr. Kendall and Shunghee that Mr. Clark must not come to N.Zealand, if they expect him to be employed

in making muskets—It will be better to settle this point with them while Mr. Clark is here. I have put him in Charge of the native Institution from the first of January where he is usefully employed, and will be no expense to the Society while he remains on that Situation—[53]

Like the Shelleys, the Clarks became deeply engrossed in their work on the 500-acre site which comprised a few sheds and one 70' long building which Clark had practically built himself. In October 1823, Clark wrote to the Society's secretary reporting progress at Black-town:

The Natives are, I believe, the poorest objects on the habitable globe. I have seen the miserable Africans first come from the holds of Slave Ships; but they do not equal in wretchedness and misery, the New Hollanders. I have in some measure been the means of removing from the minds of a few of them the prejudice excited by the Heathenish conduct of those around them calling themselves Christians, and have the pleasure of seeing ten or twelve regularly attend the Service here on the Lord's Day. We have now a commodious Mission House, with room to accommodate at least Sixty Native Children. I had 12 under my care, but one promising little Boy died. I have as good hopes respecting them, as I should have of as many European Children.[54]

At the beginning of 1824, control at Blacktown passed to the Rev. W. Walker but by the end of the year the school there had closed and the settlement was virtually abandoned. The decision to close Blacktown was made by the new government committee which had taken charge of public education including the orphanages. In the 1820s both institutions had been involved in public scandals and had continued to suffer under their customary handicaps of internal staff dissentions, exorbitant running costs, inadequate supervisory procedures and part-time committee management. Late in 1823 Brisbane had had enough and, when two vacancies occurred on the female orphan school committee, he placed a notice in *The Sydney Gazette* relieving the committee members of the orphanages and the Black Native Institution of their posts.[55] They were replaced by a committee of three including the colonial secretary and the Rev. T. Reddall whom Brisbane had appointed director-general of schools with the responsibility of re-organizing the public school system. However, before Reddall could take up his new appointment, Bathurst informed Brisbane that he had created an archdeaconship in New South Wales whose incumbent would act as King's Visitor to public schools. This appointment superseded that of the director-general. An outcome of the changes so far as the Aborigines were concerned was the removal of the boys to Liverpool, the girls going with the Rev. W. Walker to the Female Orphan School.

The incarceration of the girls in the orphanage marked yet another stage in Aboriginal education. The move had Brisbane's support, the governor contending that he was 'anxious also to try the experiment of the white and black Natives of this Colony imbibing their earliest intellectual and religious ideas under a common roof'.[56] In 1827 the girls were rescued by the newly-appointed King's Visitor, Thomas Hobbes Scott, who put both sexes in the care of CMS missionary Rev. W. Hall in a return to Blacktown. The revived institution included a number of the hardiest Maori children who had survived their stay at Marsden's Parramatta school. Scott's instructions to Hall envisaged a curriculum comprising 'the Common Elements of Education' with carpentry for boys and plain needlework for the girls;[57] and he directed the master to observe the following rules:

1. The children to be up and dressed by 6 and set to work.
2. To wash themselves at ½ past 7 go to Prayers and Breakfast at 8.
3. To work till 10 Clock.
4. To wash and go to school from 10 till 12, write one Copy read ½ an hour cypher 1 Hour.
5. To dine at ¼ after 12 and play till 1.
6. To School at 1 read & cypher till 2.
7. To work from 2 till 6 the boys at carpentering the girls sewing and knitting.
8. To play and wash and be ready for supper at 7.
9. To prayers at ½ past 7 and to be in bed at 8.
10. On Saturday morning to be devoted to instruction of Church Service.
11. The following rewards to be given in Tickets for
    1. Good Behaviour,
    2. Good Work,
    3. Religious knowledge in which they are to be examined every Sunday of one Ticket at each time at the discretion of the master and mistress and for every 10 Tickets an account shall be kept in a book entitling the children to sixpence to be laid out for their benefit at the discretion of the Visitor.[58]

Physical conditions at Blacktown were an important factor militating against the school's success. The surrounding land was insufficient for the pasture of its cattle, fresh water was a quarter of a mile away and had to be fetched by hand, and the school was robbed a number of times. In 1827 it held 'five New Zealanders and seven New Hollanders'[59] but on the removal of the Maoris Hall found it increasingly difficult to retain the others. In July 1828, he informed the archdeacon that the cattle would be better sold than kept. As things stood they were

. . . a source of trouble to the Aborigine Natives in the school, that would rather starve than do anything that has the appearance of work.
The idea of minding the cattle has driven two of the Boys away out of the School and we have none at present that we can depend upon.[60]

Other problems facing Hall were how to keep the children in bounds and how best to overcome the prejudice of Aboriginal parents who refused to have their children exposed to any formal schooling. The school became as much a holding centre for sick native children as an educational institution.

Hall supported a plan to remove the pupils to a farm where they were boarded at £25 per annum for each of ten children[61] and the Blacktown school closed for good. The decision to terminate the experiment was made primarily on economic grounds. The upkeep cost of the Blacktown school was around £1,000 a year for the accommodation of about ten pupils and when the archdeacon was forced to make drastic economies in 1828 an obvious measure was to abandon Blacktown. There was no public outcry at the decision. Unlike Shelley's school, the Blacktown institution had no spectacular successes to its credit while its failures were common property. Aborigines there were said to have worked 'like prisoners'[62] in the fields and the first lad apprenticed to learn the trade of builder promptly absconded.[63] E. S. Hall, the editor of the *Sydney Monitor*, expressed a personal view of its demise in November 1828:

The School, I believe, for the sake of *a name*, and because its public abandonment might be considered a blot on the Government in this religious age, is still alive and lingers; but its spirit, with that of its founder, is departed.[64]

If Scott had expectations of support from officialdom in England, harking back to Bathurst's earlier remarks that 'Any project for extending to them the Benefits of Civilization and Instruction' would be certain to have the 'cordial Approbation of The Prince Regent',[65] his hopes were dispelled by Viscount Goderich's instruction to Governor Darling of 6 July 1827:

. . . I need not point out to you the expediency of suspending for the present any extensive exertions, leading to expense, which it might otherwise be expedient to use in favour of the Aborigines of New South Wales. The Archdeacon's proceedings should, therefore, be confined to the obtaining of correct information as to the numbers and condition of those people.[66]

Although publicly and privately Scott had encouraged Hall during his frustrating experiences at Blacktown, the archdeacon personally doubted the feasibility of attempts to educate Aboriginal children in isolation from their families:

. . . I am thoroughly satisfied that, unless the Government are prepared to go the length of feeding and clothing the whole of them (4,500) at an immense Expense, and that constantly, not the least progress will be made either as to Civilization or Conversion. [67]

In the absence of strong motivation or surplus funds, plans for assimilating Aborigines into colonial society lapsed in favour of the more narrowly conceived object of attempting to convert selected tribes to Christianity.

Efforts by colonists to educate Aboriginal children by destroying their 'erratic' habits in homes or institutions invariably failed. While evidence was collected testifying to the ability of Aborigines to learn the skills of a servant, of rudimentary book learning or of a trade, no way was found to induce them to practise their new abilities in western society. The achievement-centred norms of the white man's world, its competitive nature and sense of the value of time and of property were alien to Aboriginal culture. To the Aboriginal child, formal education must have appeared an unreal and futile exercise. And while a few whites were patient and humane teachers of European ways many were not.

The doctrine of the noble savage which conceived the Aborigine to be in a natural state of grace did not survive colonists' observations of his actual behaviour. It was quite beyond the comprehension of men like David Collins how Aborigines 'kindly treated, fed, and often clothed' could fail to respond with 'the smallest degree of gratitude'. [68] Similarly white upholders of law and order thought it inexplicable that Aborigines could cry while watching a man justly flogged or who were so perverse as to menace the flagellator. [69] A new blood sport of pitting Aborigine against Aborigine until one lay bleeding between life and death amused the depraved and sadists encouraged Aborigines to injure themselves in tricks with gunpowder and boiling water. The inhumanities the penal settlement had brought were visited on the black equally with the white. In 1795 the Rev. T. F. Palmer described how colonists had

. . . seized a native boy who lived with a settler, and made him discover where his parents and relations concealed themselves. They came upon them unarmed, and unexpected, killed five and wounded many more. The dead they hang on gibbets, in terrorem. [70]

As the settlement expanded, clashes between Aborigines and settlers over land rights increased. Here the government's response was to permit whites the use of force in the protection of their property while urging on them the platitude of 'a great degree of forbearance and plain dealing'. [71] Aborigines were driven from their hunting grounds and thus alienated from their spiritual homeland;

they fell victims to smallpox and pneumonia; and were indiscriminately slaughtered by men 'who thought no more of shooting a native than shooting a crow'.[72] Those who regretted the noticeable decline in the numbers of the Aboriginal people by the mid-nineteenth century, were told that their objections were 'hardly more reasonable than it would be to complain of the drainage of marshes or of the disappearance of wild animals'.[73] And they were comforted by the attitude that the decimation of this people with 'No signs of any religion'[74] was an indication that the race was doomed by Providence.[75]

To the noted nineteenth-century gazetteer, J. McCulloch, the Aborigine appeared 'essentially, and not accidentally, inferior even to the lowest type of negro'.[76] McCulloch argued:

> It would be a libel on Providence, to suppose that this extensive position of the earth should be for ever occupied by a handful of naked savages, without arts, science, industry, or civilization of any kind.

So low indeed did the intellect of the Aborigine come to be rated that when the phrenological systems of Drs Gall and Spurzheim took the public's fancy

> ... the skulls of several of them were sent over to England to be submitted to the manipulations of its professors, with a view to ascertaining whether the creator had not thrust into existence a whole race of idiots—men who had neither reason to guide them on the one hand, nor well-developed instinct on the other.

The stage had been set as far back as 1799 after the white murderers of two Aboriginal boys went scot-free. Not until 1838 were white men hanged for the slaughter of Aboriginal men, women and children, and then some observers of justice done could still protest at the severity of the sentence for what was a time-honoured colonial custom.

Chapter X

SOCIAL CLASS
AND PRIVATE EDUCATION

> Generally we consider that the first class is
> Military; the second, the Civil; the third,
> the Settlers, in that class I include not only
> those from England, but those which were
> settled, and had grants after having received
> free pardons; the fourth class are called
> Landholders, they are made up of persons
> renting land, and, I believe, including some
> ticket of leave men; the fifth class, common
> labourers, free; the sixth class, ticket of leave
> men and convicts.
>
> GOVERNOR BLIGH at the
> Select Committee on Transportation,
> 1812[1]

The founding fathers of New South Wales were notorious for their
fine sense of discrimination in matters of social class. The attitude
of the self-styled gentry of Botany Bay was well illustrated in their
treatment of the Rev. H. Fulton, a priest of the Church of Ireland,
who had ministered at Norfolk Island, the Hawkesbury, Parramatta
and Sydney. While respectable colonists were prepared to receive
communion at his hands, the stigma of a prior conviction ensured
that the government-pardoned cleric was 'never received into the
class of Gentlemen'.[2] By the early 1800s a number of small private
academies had opened to meet the demands of such socially conscious parents who wanted an exclusive education for their children.

Many parents eagerly sought out a segregated schooling so that
their sons and daughters would not have to sit alongside the child
of a working convict in a public school. A parent's recognition of
social distinctions was not related solely to breeding or entry to the
colony as a free man, wealth was just as important in the business
of separating man from man. Colonists grew rich supplementing the
deficiencies of ship-carried stock, by catering for the sealers and
whalers, and in the purveying of luxuries—especially the anodyne

of Bengal rum which helped make the colonial day bearable. The cause of the colonial *entrepreneur* was abetted by English attitudes which thought it preferable for an ex-convict to make his home in the colony rather than to encourage him to return to the scene of his crime. Britons were also optimistic that one day, perhaps not too far distant, the labours of her industrious peasants and capitalists would make New South Wales financially independent of the mother country.

The officer class made the most of its opportunities to trade. Men like Lts G. Johnston, E. Abbott and J. Macarthur made small fortunes for themselves trafficking in spirits, land, sealing and sandalwood. There were pickings too for the less exalted. Sgt T. Laycock made money from land; the seaman, T. Moore, turned master boatbuilder; and the purser of the First Fleet, J. Palmer, put his capital to work in farming, shipping and flour milling. But it was not long before the emancipists and free settlers supplanted the military as the colony's Phoenicians. The ability to keep an orderly public house, operate a tannery, build a boat or a salt-manufacturing plant, edit a newspaper, bake bread and brew beer were skills which assured their ex-convict owners of a good livelihood if not a seat at every colonial table. The successes of some of them, 'the very dregs of those who have been sent here convicts',[3] led Hunter to comment to the secretary of state on over-easy routes to affluence. By way of comparison the governors themselves took home very little; it was not unknown for the man at the top to augment his salary from past gains in order to cover expenses.

Parents in New South Wales wanting the traditional start in life for their children had much to overcome. In Mrs Eliza Marsden's opinion there was 'not one good school'[4] in the colony so she taught her daughter, Anne, at home until the girl was old enough to be sent to England to school. Another dissatisfied parent was Mrs Elizabeth Macarthur who wrote to a friend in England in 1795:

> Nothing induces me to wish for a change but the difficulty of educating our children, and were it otherwise, it would be unjust towards them to confine them to so narrow a society. My desire is that they should see a little more of the world, and better learn to appreciate this retirement. Such as it is the little creatures all speak of going home to England with rapture. My dear Edward almost quitted me without a tear.[5]

In November 1801, her daughter, Elizabeth, and son, John, accompanied their father to England to school where John attended university. The Macarthurs' other sons, James and William, followed in their footsteps.

Commandant King's children, Phillip and Maria, returned home with their parents in 1797. King had hoped to leave them in England on his return to Norfolk Island but was forced to give up the idea when he became a virtual bankrupt during the long delay in fitting out his command. Promise of compensation from the Treasury arrived just in time for King to afford to have Maria board with friends and keep Phillip at Rev. P. Burford's boarding school at Stratford Green where the lad was taught Greek, Latin, French, English, writing and accounts for 10s. a week. The governor put his two illegitimate sons, Sydney and Norfolk, with a Mr Chapman in Yorkshire directing him to train them for the Navy and not to neglect the boys' religion 'notwithstanding the atheistical example of our neighbours'.[6]

One socially acceptable way of avoiding the public school was to engage a tutor or governess. Their employment had gained respectability from Locke's advice that English day schools should be shunned whatever the cost, and from Rousseau's acceptance of tutors for those parents who were sufficiently wealthy to be able to relieve themselves of the obligation of teaching their own children. For a while the Macarthurs employed a tutor, Huon de Kerilleau, a younger son of a great French family and nephew of the Bishop of St Pol who had enlisted in the New South Wales Corps.[7] The Macarthurs also engaged a governess, Miss Lucas,[8] whom they had brought out from England. Other colonists who made use of tutors were George Johnston[9] and the wife of Dr Arndell. Mrs Arndell engaged

> the notorious pickpocket Thomas Hardy Vaux as tutor, and rose early and sat up late at her domestic duties to enable her to spare the time to protect her children from the contaminating influence of a convict teacher by sitting with them throughout their lesson time.[10]

The same man was employed by Marsden to teach his children on the trip home in 1807. However, the chaplain lost Vaux's services when the convict celebrated the expiration of his sentence with a display of insubordination which required his impressment into the crew.[11]

Putting young children in the care of convicts and ex-convicts was a dubious practice. According to one parent 'they were always found to be bad subjects' and, if convict governesses were engaged, 'there was an intrigue with the son, if there was one'.[12] For many women the exchange of virtue for the hope of release from bondage must have appeared a reasonable gamble. The fact that the colonial matrimonial market favoured the single girl until well into the nineteenth century added to the shortage of suitable governesses. The local situation led one immigration adviser to the British public to advise parents intending to take servants with them to New South Wales not to select any who were 'pretty or young they are snapped up in a moment. The best thing you can do is to select some old crone, not past work, who is very ugly, and even then you must not count on keeping her for certain'.[13]

Advertisements for tutors and governesses in *The Sydney Gazette* provide some indication of demand. They also reflect on the inferior quality of many of the township's day schools; some typical objections to these were voiced by H. Kingsley in his novel *Geoffry Hamlyn*:

> " . . . his mother has taught him all she knows, so I suppose he must go to school and fight, and get flogged, and come home with a pipe in his mouth, and an oath on his lips, with his education completed. I don't fancy his staying here among these convict servants, when he is old enough to learn mischief."

> "He'll learn as much mischief at a colonial school, I expect," said the Doctor, "and more too. All the evil he hears from these fellows will be like the water on a duck's back; whereas, if you send him to school in a town, he'll learn a dozen vices he'll never hear of here. Get him a tutor."[14]

Most tutors and governesses employed by the middle ranks of society were convicts or ex-convicts and some could well have worked as teachers in England. In his study of 1,248 women convicts,[15] Dr L. L. Robson discovered three governesses: one was a nursery teacher with a prior conviction transported for stealing silver spoons; the second was sentenced for forging a cheque; and the third, also with a previous conviction, was transported for stealing a shawl. The last woman claimed teaching competencies in drawing, singing, French and fancy needle-work. Accomplishments like these had an important influence on market price. If of free-immigrant background, the better-educated governess could hope to find a place with the social *élite* who were prepared to pay well to have their daughters taught the polite subjects. However, the balance of the tutors and governesses was equated with the servant class. When agencies like the Servants' Registry Office opened in Sydney, they advertised the services of 'every description of farm and domestic servants, mechanics, educated persons and others of good character'.[16] Along with her teaching duties, a governess of this class would be expected to serve as book-keeper, secretary, domestic help, companion, letter-writer and entertainer of visitors.

If a parent was not prepared to chance sending his child to England to school, risking shipwreck at the least, or the employment of a convict tutor or governess, he had the option of patronizing one of several small academies which had sprung up in Sydney and Parramatta. These private schools were of three main types: those teaching the three Rs at minimum rates; more expensive schools offering post-elementary skills; and select academies for young ladies. The first category contained the private venture schools of the ex-convicts, 1. Nelson and T. Taber, and of D. Parnell; it also included the Perfects' Class at 6 Spring Road, Sydney, and the evening class held in R. Shreeves' house at the Rocks whose teachers had come free to the colony.[17] Their curriculum comprised the basic subjects with book-keeping and accounts usually available as extras.

The second group of schools justified its existence by claiming to teach an extensive range of post-elementary studies. These schools had affinities with the dissenters' academies in England which taught a modern curriculum and which were currently attracting pupils who would otherwise have attended the Latin grammars. In the seventeenth century Locke had attacked the predominance of Latin in schools and had formed the opinion that logic, rhetoric and Greek were often not worth teaching. The philosopher advocated a practical education arguing that learning was of worth in so far as it led to knowledge of the world.[18] A century later Benjamin Franklin in his Academy at Philadelphia took Locke's point a step further when he asserted that the job of education was 'to bake bread'.[19]

The expectation that education should be useful helped the dissenters' academies in England attract pupils to a curriculum which included subjects like geography, science and European languages. Some endowed classical schools moved to imitate them, however, they were checked by the law of the land. In a court action in 1805 Lord Eldon opposed what he saw as a plot by the managers of Leeds Grammar School to widen their curriculum to serve the business interests of the burghers of Leeds. 'It is not that the poor Inhabitants are to be taught reading and writing English', Eldon complained, but that 'the Clerks and Riders of the Merchants are to be taught French and German to carry on a Trade. I fear the effect would be to turn out the poor Latin and Greek scholars altogether'.[20] His Lordship's ruling did not, of itself, prevent curriculum reform; indeed it may have accelerated it. However, as late as the 1820s the place of Latin and Greek in any education worthy of the name was still under debate in New South Wales where the draft curriculum of the King's School, established to train Anglican leaders, could find no place for the study of English.

Probably the best of the early private academies teaching post-elementary studies was Crook's school at Parramatta where pupils could learn 'to read, speak, and write the English Tongue with accuracy and propriety, Book-keeping, Geometry, Trigonometry, and Mensuration, practically applied in Navigation, Surveying, Gauging, etc.'[21] A second academy offering post-elementary subjects was run in Sydney by J. Mitchell and J. MacConnell who, taking 'every pains' with their pupils, taught 'English grammatically, Writing, Book-keeping after the Italian mode, French grammatically, and Mathematics'.[22] There were clients, too, for Howe's after-hours class which followed the practical curriculum of

> ... Simple, Vulgar and Decimal Arithmetic, Mensuration, many useful Arithmetical Abbreviations, Writing (if necessary); and the Grammar of the English Tongue upon the Principles of Drs. Lowth, Johnson, Priestly, & other celebrated Writers who have united their efforts in improving the Grammatical structure of their own beautiful and comprehensive Language, which every Englishman ought to be acquainted with, but few attain that have not had the advantage of a classical education.[23]

Although Howe carried a palm for the classics, he made no attempt to teach them himself. This may be attributed to gaps in his own learning but such deficiencies had never prevented other masters from laying claims to expertise in subject areas of which they knew little if the skills appeared saleable. A paragraph in another advertisement carried in Howe's paper, with its claim to teach a curriculum 'adapted to the Situation for which the Pupil may be designed',[24] suggests a more plausible reason. Latin, Greek and Hebrew were simply not offered in these schools because the public demand was overwhelmingly for useful subjects. Colonial teachers were forced to justify post-elementary studies on the grounds that they led to useful knowledge like 'accompts' or 'Mensuration, practically applied', and they did not waste time arguing a case for scholarship in its own right. William Maum, the convict teacher at Parramatta, who was described as 'Teacher of Latin and Greek'[25] in the ship's indents, made no attempts to advertise his accomplishments. Nor did any other teacher before 1810.

At this time no distinction existed between elementary and secondary education. Private schoolmasters still met their basic costs by teaching the skills of literacy; and the private pupil typically began his schooldays in the alphabet class working his way as far as his master could take him or until his parents lost patience with his schooling and put him to work. Severe organizational problems were posed for headmasters in these days by the unavoidable intermingling of young children and adolescents under one teacher in the one classroom.

In 1803 'Incognito' argued in *The Sydney Gazette* that there could be no improvement in colonial private schooling until two grades of academies were introduced. Under the existing system the older child was retarded 'by a want of inducement and a spur to emulation', while the younger found himself 'stigmatized with the want of natural talent which only lies concealed because it is not courted'.[26] He proposed a system of dual academies: one for 'the most advanced Youth only'; and the second taught by a 'plain Teacher' who would relieve academicians of 'the extreme drudgery of making the first impression on the infant understanding'.

The introduction of post-elementary studies brought new textbooks to the colony. The most numerous of these were the English grammars, which were playing an important part in making English teaching acceptable through the application of the principles of Latin analysis and by re-prints of elegant extracts from English literature by authors like Pope, Addison and Swift which they presented for study and imitation. The best known of them was Lindley Murray's *English Grammar* first published in 1795.

Young readers working their way through Murray's book were urged to impress 'piety and virtue' on their minds and were cautioned against becoming

> . . . absorbed in over-curious or trifling speculations; if your heart and principles be debased and poisoned, by the influence of corrupting and pernicious books, for which no elegance of composition can make amends; if you spend so much of your time in literary engagements, as to make them interfere with higher occupations, and lead you to forget, that pious and benevolent action is the great end of your being: if such be the unhappy misapplication of your acquisitions and advantages,— instead of becoming a blessing to you, they will prove the occasion of greater condemnation; and, in the hour of serious thought, they may excite the painful reflections,—that it would have been better for you, to have remained illiterate and unaspiring; to have been confined to the humblest walks of life; and to have been even hewers of wood and drawers of water all your days.[27]

Professional reviewers of *English Grammar* thought the work 'the best in the English language', a book of 'inestimable utility' and one especially serviceable to foreigners. Its author, they claimed, was entitled to 'public protection' and the 'gratitude of every friend to English literature, and to true virtue'.[28] A close friend of Murray's is the sole objector remembered. He informed the author that 'Of all contrivances invented for puzzling the brains of the young your grammar is the worst'.[29] Nonetheless the book was in heavy demand as fodder in the battle for the improvement of children's minds and thirty-seven editions had been printed by 1824.

Other texts finding a market were geographies with notes on

air, soil, political boundaries, products and national characteristics in which non-English ways of living were compared unfavourably with institutions like the Established Church, parliamentary government and the fighting qualities of John Bull. More specialized textbooks were also beginning to appear in the general stores. The book-buying public could order treatises on mathematics, music and song books, and works on political science and physiology. However, the age of popular reading had not yet dawned. Books remained comparatively expensive in the colony and the demand for fiction had not made bookrooms or public lending libraries feasible.

By the late eighteenth century authors and schoolmasters were becoming aware of the quicker learning accruing from lively text-books and the returns this meant in sales. J. Newbery had consider-able success with his *A Little Pretty Pocket Book* in 1774 which contained amusement rhymes designed as aids in learning the alphabet:

> So great O, and P,
> Pray what do you see?
> *A naughty boy whipt;*
> But that is not me.[30]

Newbery's imitators joined the Rouseauphiles in a movement to make learning a more pleasurable experience which had some influence in the colony. Johnson collected a bulk shipment of *Reading Made Easy*[31] for use in his public schools and Crook wrote home for supplies of 'pleasing as well as edifying reading books'[32] for his Sydney academy. By the early nineteenth century advertisers in *The Sydney Gazette* were publicizing 'improved'[33] plans of education and were arguing for 'well-adapted Proverbs'[34] as the quickest route to learning in schemes designed to make 'every part of Education as pleasing as possible'.[35]

By the 1800s quantities of children's books mostly didactic in tone were being imported into New South Wales. A popular author of books for children, J. Janeway, explained to his young readers that 'Hell is a terrible place, that's worse a thousand times than whipping' but for those children who attain Heaven 'they shall never be beat any more, they shall never be sick, or in pain any more'.[36] The moralists of the Janeway breed rejected content drawn from English folk stories because they considered it unwholesome. John Marshall, author of seventy children's books between 1780 and 1790, made his money from works 'entirely divested of that prejudicial Nonsense (to young Minds) the Tales of Hobgoblins, Witches, Fairies, Love, Gallantry, etc., with which such little Performances heretofore abounded'.[37] One arbiter of middle-class decencies went so far as to condemn Cinderella as 'one of the most exceptionable books that was ever written for children . . . It paints some of the worst passions that can enter into the human breast, and of which little children should, if possible, be totally ignorant; such as envy, jealousy, a dislike to mothers-in-law and half-sisters, vanity, a love of dress'.[38] Bowdlerized literature of this kind was thought especially suitable for girls.

Women's rights led by that 'hyena in petticoats',[39] Mary Wollstonecraft, made considerable gains in England towards the end of the eighteenth century. Dr Johnson, who could recall days when a woman who could spell was thought accomplished, remonstrated that blue-stockings now 'vied with the men in everything'.[40] Some progress was evident in education where women were attacking the limitations of a curriculum of drawing, painting, fancy needlework and music taught in boarding schools which were the successors of the pre-Reformation nunneries. But seeking change in the curriculum was not the prerogative of ardent feminists alone. Social conservatives, too, rejected an education dedicated to accomplishments. Their idea of a good education for girls was one devoted to the production of 'obedient Daughters, faithful Wives, and prudent Mothers . . . serviceable in domestic, and agreeable in social life'.[41] And they wanted their women 'hardily bred, not only for their own health, but to have a healthy offspring'. Of course, girls with working-class backgrounds had no place in these curriculum reforms, they were considered fortunate if they could read a simple text. In the industrial centres the demand for child labour was indifferent to sex and, in rural areas where a family's income partly depended on cottage labour, the only chance for a young girl to learn anything was to read aloud to her as her fingers worked ceaselessly at her taskwork.

The early shiploads of convict women were 'in general received rather as prostitutes than as servants'.[42] Not until 1800, when two colonial matrons were officially appointed to the orphan school committee, did colonial womanhood publically emerge from its condition of semi-official concubinage. In the decade that followed, half-a-dozen day schools opened exclusively for girls which differed from the boys' academies both in staffing and curricula. Headmistresses of these private girls' schools were not convicts or ex-convicts and their press advertisements made strong selling points of their ability to teach 'virtuous precepts'.[43] Like the boys' academies, these schools offered the basic subjects; however, their extras were 'fine Needlework, Marking, Tambour work',[44] 'external manners'[45] and 'Accompts'.[46] In offering 'Accompts', colonial headmistresses broke with English tradition for it was not considered respectable there for young ladies to work for a living. At least no local headmistress was sufficiently vulgar as to detail her fees in an advertisement although one did pluck up courage to hint that hers, 'she flatters herself will not be considered exhorbitant'.[47] Places at the select academies of Mesdames Marchant, Hodges and Perfect were in demand and the girls' schools achieved a continuity of operation which eluded many of their masculine counterparts.

Something of the risks and profits for a schoolmistress were evident in the career of Mrs Marchant who arrived in the colony in 1807 with her husband to take charge of the female orphan school. Four months later Mr Marchant was shot dead. What happened was described by the widow in a laconic statement to the secretary of state

> . . . the Wretched Man who shot him held his Blunderbuss close to him, the Ball went through just under the Shoulder Bone; he did not survive but a short time. I feel particularly happy, the Almighty bless'd him with his senses to the last; he told who the Man was . . . I was in Bed, on Mr. Marchant crying *Murder*, I rush'd from my Room amongst the fire and smoke, and cried Murder; till I alarm'd the Camp. Lieut. Bragbout and a file of Men, came to my assistance and the Wretched Man was taken and put in Irons.[48]

Mrs Marchant's trauma did not upset her composure or her determination to make a success of her new life. Within a few years the eligible widow had married again and was proprietor of a popular ladies' academy in Sydney.

From the very beginning, proprietors of private schools had received a share of the public resources. The governor helped them with plots of land, an assignee or two and the occasional use of a government building. Teachers were also encouraged to emigrate to New South Wales. Sir Joseph Banks was approached by one English schoolmaster, W. Coe, with an offer to open an academy in New South Wales for the colony's 'respectable Settlers'.[49] His price was 500 acres of land, ten cows at the government rate, four convicts on the stores for eighteen months, a Sydney house and a free passage out for a family of four all rationed for eighteen months. The terms were not taken up. They contrasted with the usual government inducement for an emigrant teacher without capital of 50 acres and one assignee.

The governors directly associated themselves with the educational exertions of the owners of private schools through an annual inspection of proprietors and pupils at government house. The practice had its beginnings in attempts to assure 'both the Parent and Preceptor that the British Legislature is sincerely interested in the improvement of its Youth, it is to be hoped a sense of duty to their Country, their

Children, and their God, will prevent any relaxation in the exertion necessary to the desirable attainment of a moral and religious education'.[50] These examinations began under Hunter who made it a rule

> . . . to see the children every year regularly, and they were all brought up, boys and girls, with their masters and mistresses, and produced specimens of the improvements they had made, to me, which I kept, and compared when I next saw them.[51]

The link between private enterprise and the government in education was strengthened by Bligh when he instructed chaplain Fulton 'to attend to all the private schools, to see that they were regulated'.[52] The arrangement lasted until the onset of the Rum Rebellion.

Despite the varied means of official encouragement, colonial parents considered that the private academies to which they had access were inferior in quality to those of England. They complained that imported brains were invariably superior to local talent for whom 'the season of improvement has been suffered to glide imperceptibly by',[53] and they were concerned for the future should the colony's infant geniuses 'still be permitted to slumber in the chambers of ignorance and indifference'. Although private schools received liberal government aid,[54] several of their teachers showed little interest in their work. Inquisitive Observer writing in *The Sydney Gazette* attributed this to the state of affairs where pupils were often several quarters fees in arrears and a master's income seldom reached 10s. a week. 'Alas! poor pedant!', lamented this friend of teachers, 'if thou wert better rewarded, thou wouldst better endeavour to deserve thy mite'.[55]

Largely irrespective of quality, the luxury of a bought education was preferred by those with money above a government-subsidized public schooling supervised by a clergyman. It was not that parents objected to turning the colonial treasury to their personal advantage but rather that many preferred exclusiveness for its own sake. In 1829 the well-intentioned Archdeacon Scott was to attempt to establish a public grammar school but because the good man refused in conscience to 'exclude a child from those benefits . . . because the Parents were humble or immoral . . . the upper classes objected to send their Children to this School'.[56] Yet the same upper classes, he protested, did not hesitate to send their sons to small private academies kept by teachers

> . . . of the most worthless character, who had formerly been Convicts and who were notorious drunkards, who felt no remorse at the introduction of Spirits amongst the Children of the School, when both the latter and the former equally participated in these libations; the consequences

as were anticipated have indeed been lamentable. It is nevertheless a notorious fact that these persons have not only been patronized most openly and confidentially by high influential persons in the Colony, but Parents have actually taken their Children from the more reputable masters and placed them under these vicious and immoral Teachers, alleging that the Schools were more convenient to their dwellings, the distance in neither case exceeding a quarter of a mile.

In centres where only a teacher in receipt of government assistance was available, a canvas tarpaulin was sometimes strung across the classroom to divide the children of convicts from those of fee-paying parents.

However, it would be an over-simplification to attribute parental preference for a private schooling solely to a demand for social status. For well-educated parents the difficulties faced in bringing up their children were a major hardship attached to pioneering a new land. They watched dismayed as their families grew up unable to benefit from the kind of experiences which had formed their own backgrounds. As one such parent explained:

> . . . the welfare of my uninstructed child goes near to my heart, and instead of being able to direct and look after her I am obliged to perform the most menial offices.[57]

At least in an alien land, educated parents had the residue of their own schooling, something to look back upon and to set a standard of acceptable conduct among gentlefolk. But their children often had only what could be passed on to them in their less-crowded hours. As J. C. Ross observed in Van Diemen's Land:

> It was quite distressing to witness the contrast between the English educated parents and their grown-up children, whose manners and ideas seemed barely equal to those of the lower uneducated order of society at home.[58]

In the bush children were isolated in an adult world among companions who were often ticket-of-leave men or assigned convicts. While in the townships their environment included the sight of flogging and the sounds of screams and blasphemies, they saw drunkards in stocks, convicts working in chains and public executions. Parents might be prosperous but for all that their money could not buy them the education they so desired for their children.

Chapter XI

EDUCATIONAL TRADITION
AND A CONVICT COLONY

> God is from these very stones, from the
> sweepings of Jails, hulks and brothels,
> raising up children unto Abraham.

MARSDEN, 4 June 1819[1]

As the *Buffalo* tacked through Sydney Heads on the 28 September
1800, Hunter and Johnson, both homeward bound, could have
congratulated themselves that more children attended school in
New South Wales in proportion to the child population than were
in attendance in many English counties. Most were enrolled in
public elementary schools, a fact which contrasted with the practices
in other British possessions where grammar schools for the well-to-do
were often established before elementary schools. For inspiration
colonists had drawn on their homeland experiences. Women had
been encouraged to open small schools, the church school in Hyde
Park had its affinities with England's parochial and charity schools,
and religious content was taught in colonial classrooms under the
supervision of the clergy of the Church of England using teaching
methods common throughout Britain.

But of equal importance in understanding colonial education
were the innovations which departed radically from English custom.
In New South Wales the clergy acted at the governor's behest, they
were effectively isolated from powerful ecclesiastical superiors and
the teachers they supervised were mostly untrained ex-convicts
working in makeshift accommodation. These public schoolmasters
were dependent on government paternalism for their survival. It
was the governor who directed that convict labour be released for
teaching, that schoolmasters be rationed from the stores, and who
rewarded them with land grants and assignees of their own according
to his view of their deserts. Support from the government relieved
them of the necessity of depending upon fees for a living and with
this came the responsibility of providing a free education for the
children of the poor.

To have improved on English education at the turn of the nineteenth century could conceivably have committed colonists to a system like that introduced in Prussia in 1763 which decreed the compulsory attendance at school of children from five to thirteen years, the organization of schools including textbooks, discipline and the order of exercises, and which fined parents who kept their children at home.[2] Britons, however, put less trust in the state than did continentals, and their efforts were as much directed at inhibiting as encouraging state aid. Opponents of state intervention argued that a network of schools could provide a channel for the spread of seditious ideas, and that the dissemination of education among all social classes would lead to a shortage of manual labourers and would increase proportionately 'the classes of men that live on the labour of others'.[3] It is fair to say that Britons had clearer ideas about what the state should not do, than what it should attempt. Hence few were surprised when Whitbread's bill to provide a system of elementary education throughout the country in 1807 was soundly defeated in the Lords.[4]

Although New South Wales had more to offer than the educational wasteland that was late eighteenth-century England, colonial education itself lessened in effectiveness after 1800. The decline was related to the increase in the child population on the mainland which almost doubled to reach just on 1,800 between 1800-6,[5] as well as to the dispersed nature of the settlement. At its most spectacular the physical expansion of the colony had seen limpet ports bud along the east coast of the continent. In 1801 a settlement was made at Coal River north of Sydney; and two years later a party camped at Risdon Cove, Van Diemen's Land. In 1804 a second group settled at Sullivan Cove on the Derwent; and that year a party from Norfolk Island established Port Dalrymple. The progress of education in these various settlements was a chancy affair. There were over fifty children in the Launceston district by 1809[6] but no school had opened for them.

When considering the adequacy of public education these romantic re-creations of 1788 were of less significance than the shifts of population on the mainland. The earliest centres of educational activity were at Sydney and Parramatta which were the headquarters of the colonial administration, the permanent stations of the chaplains and busy trading centres and ports for their surrounding districts. However, the mobility of their populations must have retarded many a child's progress at school. Between 1792-6 the population of Parramatta virtually halved following reductions in the military garrison and as people flocked to the newly-opened Hawkesbury River flats.[7] Phillip had explored the Hawkesbury as early as 1789 but six years were to elapse before boats plying the route via Broken Bay to Port Jackson helped make settlement there an economic proposition. In June 1795, some 500 settlers were farming the fertile northern and southern flats of the river and its tributaries.[8] By then farmers had also clustered on the pockets of better soil in the Sydney hinterland. They were cultivating the Ponds district north east of Parramatta, Prospect Hill to the west, Toongabbie north of Prospect and Field of Mars east of the Ponds; and there were settlements north of the harbour at Kissing Point and Hunter's Hill.

Assuming that a man working a farm at an outer settlement was prepared to reduce the labour at his command by permitting his child to attend school, the physical difficulties of attendance often put insuperable obstacles in the way. A child must get to school as best he could on foot for a horse was a luxury few parents of public school children could afford. Admittedly Parramatta and Sydney had been connected by bush track and water virtually from the beginning. A carriage road to the Hawkesbury was cut as early as 1795[9] and a system of roads linked Sydney with Parramatta and the Hawkesbury via Toongabbie and Prospect, with branch routes connecting Sydney and the Hawkesbury via Liverpool by 1806. However, many outlying properties were not linked by the main arteries which themselves were not much more than bridle-paths deeply rutted by ox-wagons. While the northern harbour settlements were only readily accessible by water and children must commute by ferry to attend school in Sydney or Parramatta.

Nor was it just the physical difficulties which often made schooling impracticable: poverty, too, stopped schools opening. The government's policy of making small land grants, many as little as ten acres, was not justified in practice. Grants changed hands continually, bankruptcies were common and men failed not for want of hard work but because of insufficient capital and inadequate knowledge of the soil and climate. Colonists beggared themselves in attempts to become farmers, or found themselves tied in a state of virtual serfdom to plots which drew them inexorably into debt. Where the soil was poorest, demoralized farmers eked out the barest of livings and some were dependent on their children's labour to attain even marginal productivity. Ill-fed and scantily clothed they lived out miserable lives in the decayed and ramshackle huts of Seven Hills, Toongabbie and Baulkam Hills. Between the pockets of closer settlements were the grazing ranges where pastoralists ran sheep and cattle. These were the last districts of the hinterland to provide facilities for education.

Schools outside Sydney and Parramatta did not follow necessarily from the presence in a district of sufficient children to form a class. Influential factors in the determination of whether a school opened or not were the concentration of the population, its wealth, local geography and communications. Parental attitudes were also important as were seasonal demands for labour in the fields and the out-of-doors climate which would have made regular attendance in crowded and poorly-ventilated classrooms a severe punishment There were public schools at Kissing Point and Toongabbie before 1800 but no school at the colony's third largest settlement, Green Hills, before 1803 or at Wilberforce until 1807.[10] The Kissing Point school had much to do with missionary activity, the Toongabbie class served the workforce of a large government farm, while the Wilberforce school followed a schoolmaster taking up a grant in the district. Where there was no direct interest or profit motive operating schools came late.

To some extent education in New South Wales was encouraged by the absence of a strong demand for child labour from local industry; and it is conceivable that the shortage of skills, and hence their greater rewards, may have induced parents to keep their children at school longer. However, too much emphasis should not be placed on the notion of education as investment at this time. Certainly developments in warfare and navigation, and the growth of printing, map-making and clockmaking had stimulated the demand for literate craftsmen throughout western Europe, but these skills and the higher clerical ones remained the prerogative of a comparatively small group largely capable of meeting the demands put upon it. It was signficant that in the middle of the nineteenth century, after more than a century of rapid industrial growth, England could still operate effectively with a population only two-thirds literate.[11] Not until the 1870s did the economic growth arising from the efforts of apprentices and amateur scientists need to be replaced by an organized technology. Some idea of the restricted outlets for literacy skills in New South Wales can be gauged from the collection of the government revenue where the entire operation was managed by the naval officer and a convict clerk relying on single-entry book-keeping.

No strong ideological thrust for the implementation of a comprehensive system of education came from England on the colony's foundation. But soon afterwards the monitorial schemes of the Anglican Dr Andrew Bell and the Quaker Joseph Lancaster were to make mass elementary education feasible by their very cheapness. Under the monitorial system the schoolmaster first taught the brighter older pupils who in turn were set to teaching the lower grades; if a boy failed to maintain his lead he was demoted. Its exponents claimed that using their methods a single trained teacher could manage 500 or more pupils at an annual cost per child unit of 7s. 6d. On hearing the news George III replied 'Good' and the British public agreed.[12] By 1820 nearly a quarter of a million school children were enrolled in monitorial schools on their way to becoming 'good scholars, good men, and good Christians'.[13]

The powerful Anglican National Society for the Education of the Poor in the Principles of the Established Church adopted the scheme which Bell had expounded in his pamphlet *An Analysis of the Experiment in Education Made at Egmore, near Madras.* The doctor had aimed

> . . . to form such scholars as the condition of that country required, as were wanted to fill the various occupations which presented themselves in the existing state of things; to imbue the minds of my pupils with the principles of morality, and of our holy religion, and infuse a spirit and habit of diligence and industry; so as at once to supply the necessities of the community, and promote the welfare of the individual; two objects indissolubly united in every well regulated state.[14]

The dissenter equivalent of the National Society was the British and Foreign Schools Society based on the rival scheme of Lancaster. Both societies issued elaborate manuals on precisely how every child was to stand and sit when learning from his work cards, on what sized leather ticket must be worn on the breast from monitor-general downward, and which particular form of religious instruction was essential for his salvation. Both sets of teachers were cautioned against departing from the efficient simplicity of their system.

The new teaching system was a distinct improvement on the 'individual' method. It made possible the division of a school into small groups and, with its emphasis on competition spurred by rewards and public disgrace, the system reduced reliance on threats of hellfire and beatings in the maintenance of order in the classroom. New South Wales first heard of monitorial teaching as a method of classroom management rather than the *raison d'être* for a scheme of mass education. Crook used the Lancastrian plan in his Sydney school and modified versions were tried in some public schools; while in Macquarie's governorship, the Methodists Bowden and Hosking attempted it in the orphanages. In 1820 Rev. T. Reddall was sent from England to establish the National System in the colony and the same Anglican scheme was selected by Bigge as the basis for a complete re-organization of public education.[15] Neither monitorial system operated with much success. Both were vulnerable to sectarian objections and parents held that if their children knew enough to act as monitors they deserved to be paid for their skills or else released to earn money for their families.

The extent to which colonial education changed individual lives for the better, ameliorated colonial society or increased the productivity of the workforce cannot be assessed accurately in retrospect. Nevertheless, it seems probable that changes in literacy levels in New South Wales in the early years can be attributed in part to the schooling received by several hundred youngsters from 1792 on. A count of marriage registers taken by Mr V. Goodin[16] at St Philip's, Sydney, St John's, Parramatta, and St Matthew's, Windsor, for the years 1804 and 1814 reveals that 55 per cent. of men and 24 per cent. of women born outside the colony could sign their names, the balance marking the register 'X'. This percentage can be compared with the figure of 63 per cent. of men and 44 per cent. of women born in the colony who signed the registers over the same period. By 1821-4, of those born in the colony, 86 per cent. of men and 75 per cent. of women signed at Sydney, 80 per cent. and 79 per cent. at Parramatta, and 47 per cent and 53 per cent at Windsor. The Windsor percentages were probably influenced by outer-settlement marriages and the sparcity of the schools in these districts.

Arguments against attributing rising literacy rates solely to schooling relate to the largely unknown influence of informal routes to learning. Some colonists would have learned to read and write at home. Others may have been motivated to become literate by events about them, from opportunities for better employment, or by the stimulation of the publication of books like Thomas Paine's *Rights of Man*. There are problems, too, in identifying literacy, of how to accredit the shadow ground between competency in written language and a stumbling recitation from a simple text. But granted these qualifications it appears reasonable to argue that the long tradition of schooling in New South Wales contributed its measure to the comparatively high level of literacy among the native born.

The native born appeared remarkable in several ways. Not only were they more literate but they were generally held in higher regard in society and had a lower crime rate than convicts, emancipists and free immigrants. Apparently the first generation of currency lads and lasses mostly turned out law-abiding, sober and self-respecting citizens. Bigge, in his report on the state of the colony published in 1822-3, made the point that marriages between the native-born youth and the women convicts were rare. He attributed this

> ... chiefly to a sense of pride in the native-born youths, approaching to contempt for the vices and depravity of the convicts, even when manifested in the persons of their own parents.[17]

The commissioner recommeded that the native born become eligible for land grants and loans of cattle, and that they be accepted for jury service.

A second opinion from the 1820s was given by Peter Cunningham who informed the British reading public that her 'cornstalks' were

> . . . the theme of universal praise; and indeed, what more can be said in favour, than that they are little tainted with the vices so prominent among their parents! Drunkenness is almost unknown with them, and honesty proverbial; the few of them that have been convicted having acted under the bad auspices of their parents or relatives . . .
>
> The young girls are of mild-tempered, modest disposition, possessing much simplicity of character; and, like all children of nature, credulous and easily led into error. The lower classes are anxious to get into respectable service, from a laudable wish to be independent, and escape from the tutelage of their often profligate parents.[18]

High opinions of the native born were also held in some quarters in Britain. The correspondent in the *Edinburgh Review* of 1828 who described them as 'in a more than ordinary degree, temperate and honest',[19] indicated that their qualities were at variance with what one would expect. His testimony also stood against a theory that the white race tended to deteriorate physically and morally in the Australian climate.[20]

Evidence that the native born was the least criminal class in the colony is based on an analysis of the figures of various committals to Sydney Gaol between 1833-6 by Professor R. Ward and Mr K. Macnab, which provides an average index of 10.4 committals per 1,000 convicts, 15.4 for emancipists, 4.23 for free emigrants, and 3.43 for the native born.[21] Sir W. W. Burton, judge of the Supreme Court, was sufficiently impressed by the association of the native born and the law to comment:

> . . . there was not one of them ever tried before the writer for any of those atrocious crimes which are attributed to their country, but belong only to the convict class; nor did he hear or know of any person born in the colony, being tried for, or even charged with, either the offence of rape, or any other licentious crime; nor has he ever found any offence committed by any one of them, such as to call upon him to pronounce sentence of death; and no such sentence has ever passed within his knowledge, or any crime committed with such a degree of violence as to justify it.[22]

One can only speculate as to whether the schooling the native born received contributed to the reputation of this 'fine and manly race'.[23]

Viewed from another position Lang described young uneducated colonists as 'giddy and frivolous' showing 'a blustering and somewhat offensive affection of liberty and independence'.[24] In similar vein his Anglican co-religious Rev. William Woolls claimed that the uneducated native born were '*mad dogs* let loose upon society—they are *wild beasts* scouring the land'.[25] Both accepted that their failings followed from lamentable ignorance which Woolls thought 'the primary source of all crimes and wickedness which abound amongst us'.[26] The antidote offered by Lang in his Australian College and Woolls at the King's School, Parramatta, was a restricted form of political socialization whereby the colonial *élite* learned its role of community leadership. Lang was no advocate of education for all, and, when Woolls was stirred to comment on mass elementary education, it was to reassure the public that far from

> . . . raising the lower orders to a station not intended for them by Providence, or of causing them to entertain feelings of contempt towards their superiors, it has taught them to do their duty in that state of life to which it has pleased God to call them, and to render that respect to those in authority which religion and reason require.[27]

Undoubtedly the most formative experience on the native born was the opportunity to earn an honest living. When a child entered his teens he was regarded by official statistics as a man and by then could well have had working experience as a stockman, tradesman's assistant or bullock driver.[28] Contact with the classroom in a lad's coming-of-age was typically brief but it was one route to literacy. Some few were emphatic that its influence went much further. Marsden informed a friend in England in 1816 that he did not think 'there is any part of the world where the common People's children are so well instructed as they are here'. He linked his claim with the statement that he felt 'much pleasure in seeing the young men of the colony, tho' born of the most depraved parents, in general sober, honest and industrious'.[29]

On 24 January 1809, Isaac Lyons and John Hosking, the first trained schoolmasters with salaries paid by the British treasury disembarked from the *Aeolus*, and they were joined in 1812 by a third trained man, Thomas Bowden. With their appointment colonial schoolmasters attained the status of members of the regular civil establishment for the first time. Much of the credit for their engagement must go to Marsden who gained the ear of an influential audience on his visit to England in 1807 by disclosing the colonial census returns which listed a high proportion of illegitimate births.[30] The chaplain described the native born as 'Remote, helpless, distressed and Young, these are truly the Children of the State'.[31] His circle listened to a detailed exposition of the human condition of this 'rising Generation of several Hundreds of fine Children exposed to a contamination fatal to Body and Soul'; and they heard Marsden argue that 'wise political arrangements, good example and Christian Knowledge' were essential if 'the young of both Sexes' were to be salvaged from the destruction threatening them. On the chaplain's estimates a schoolmaster was urgently required for the Hawkesbury and Nepean settlements, two at Parramatta and at least one at Sydney. Private schoolmasters, Marsden asserted, could be obtained for the price of a free passage and a grant of land but not experienced masters and mistresses 'who shall be employed in training and, teaching the Orphans, the Children of Convicts and poor Settlers'. This 'imperious necessity' demanded a direct grant from the 'Mother Country'.

Marsden wanted schoolmaster emigrants who would 'not expect to be stationary and quiet' with constitutions strong enough to endure 'the fatigue of active Service', and having the attributes of 'personal Piety and an earnest desire to communicate Christian Knowledge'. In the absence of such qualities he considered they might as well stay at home. The chaplain had a firm ally in Wilber-force who inadvertently strengthened his pleas by mistakenly informing the British authorities that in New South Wales there were 'not 100 children who receive any education at all'.[32] In fact around 400 children were enrolled in colonial schools.

After much lobbying Marsden obtained three salaried posts from the Crown, two at £60 per annum and a third at £100. An account of the second stage of his recruitment programme was included in a letter to Hassall of 30 March 1808:

I have been down in Yorkshire, but could only stay a few days, my Business required my Attention in London—I left Mrs. Marsden in Hull, and did not see her for three months—She arrived in London on Saturday last again; I intend to leave town in about ten days, if possible having got on very well with my Affairs with Government—Two Clergymen were ordained on Sunday last who will come out before, or with me when we return—I am now looking out for another—Two or three School-masters I hope to meet with, who will be very useful in the Colony—if proper men can be found who will go—

. . .Two Schoolmasters will come likewise in her—one for the Orphan House—a Mr. Hosking and his wife pious people, and I think will answer well for that Situation—I will thank you to pay them any little Attention you can, and give them any needful Advice—the other man and his wife are not religious—but the Salary was too small for any proper person to accept it—I have met with another pious man who will probably come out in the next Ship as a Schoolmaster—when I come myself I hope to arrange things so for the Education of the Children, that most of them in the Colony may receive Instruction—[33]

Hosking was to teach at the female orphan school for nine years and Bowden took charge of the male orphanage when it opened in 1819 and managed it until 1825. But Lyons, whose wife had died on the passage out, lasted only nine months. On Marsden's evidence he 'turned out a bad character'[34] and was dismissed for incompetence by the public ignominy of a General Order on 29 October 1809:

> ISAAC LYONS having from Negligence and Incapacity proved himself totally unfit for the Situation of Schoolmaster at Parramatta, he is suspended from this Duty; and R. JONES will take Charge of the School until further Orders.[35]

A parliamentary salary and previous teaching experience set Lyons, Hosking and Bowden apart from the twenty or so men and women who had taught in public schools since 1792. Their appointments also introduced a new grade to the ranks of the existing teachers known as 'the upper class of schoolmasters'[36] and the 'Government Licensed School Masters'[37] to distinguish them from their convict or emancipist fellows. Macquarie was to establish three more of these £60 and above positions, however, he was not able to recruit trained teachers in sufficient numbers to reduce the overwhelming predominance of convict and ex-convict teachers in the school system. Of thirteen public school schoolmasters teaching outside the orphanages in 1820, only two had come to the colony free men. A generation later ex-convicts were still to be found teaching in colonial schools.

Time was running our for the military junta when the English teachers took up their posts. Macquarie was proclaimed governor on 1 January 1810, and, unprompted by clerical advisers or Whitehall, he acted immediately to extend colonial public education. Macquarie's policy of establishing charity schools in all major townships staffed by government schoolmasters teaching in government-subsidized buildings was essentially a systematic re-iteration of earlier attempts to link social reform with the provision of widespread elementary education based on Christian knowledge. The new administration was showing that it too prized schools for their social consequences. In most centres the buildings were to have the dual function of school and chapel of the Church of England.

Setting up a comprehensive system of charity schools proved more difficult than Macquarie had supposed. It appears that the working classes of New South Wales had taken advantage of an independence arising from a demand for their labour and were not disposed to bolster what sounded like a form of colonial pauperism.

The recipients of government beneficence proved ungrateful. Much difficulty was found in enrolling sufficient children for a class in Sydney and it was ten years in temporary premises before the foundation stone of a permanent building was laid. At the delayed ceremony, the government dropped the title Charity in favour of The Georgian Public School, in honour of King George III, 'the friend of piety, virtue, and literature' who, according to his colonial representatives, 'ever expressed and manifested a sincere regard for learning and science, and particularly for the christian education of youth, wishing "that every poor child throughout his dominions might be able to read the Bible"'.[38] The charity school movement, launched with high hopes and extravagant promised, soon petered out and colonial education did not move forward again until Archdeacon Scott absorbed the system into his Church and School Lands Corporation.

The pattern of education which Macquarie inherited was markedly different from other known systems. This alliance of government, church and community had had its moments of glory when local schooling had met the demands placed upon it. But more important still was the establishment of precedents which helped determine an educational tradition for the years ahead. When Sir Henry Parkes, premier of New South Wales and chief architect of the Public Instruction Act of 1880, read out two generations later that 'school-houses were built at the public expense in every village at the beginning of the Century . . . free schools were also liberally endowed, the education of neither rich nor poor being neglected',[39] the premier was paying his tribute to the varied and generous traditions of the men and women whose works have been more commonly associated with the travail and barbarities of an eighteenth-century convict colony.

NOTES

Abbreviations

ADB	*Australian Dictionary of Biography*
BSP	*British Sessional Papers*
BT	Bonwick Transcripts
CO	Colonial Office
G&GO	Government and General Order
HC	House of Commons
HRA	*Historical Records of Australia*
HRNSW	*Historical Records of New South Wales*
HSANZ	*Historical Studies, Australia and New Zealand*
JRAHS	*Journal of the Royal Australian Historical Society*
LMS	London Missionary Society
LRCS	Letters Received Colonial Secretary
LSCS	Letters Sent Colonial Secretary
ML	Mitchell Library, Sydney
PRO	Public Record Office
NSWSA	New South Wales State Archives
SC	*Select Committee*
SG	*The Sydney Gazette*
SPG	Society for the Propagation of the Gospel

Chapter I

1 J. Cobley, *Sydney Cove 1788*, London 1962, p.14.

2 CO201/2, Ross to Stephens, 13.4.1787, p.299 (PRO).

3 CO201/2, Jones to Nepean, 5.4.1787, p.295.

4 CO201/2, Sydney to Phillip, 20.4.1787, pp.132-3.

5 CO201/2, Thomas to Ross, 19.4.1787, p.308.

6 Error in addition by treasury official. CO201/8, Copy no.6, Slops Office, 27.8.1793, p.267.

7 W. Tench, *Sydney's First Four Years*, Sydney 1961, note 1, p.83.

8 CO201/4, List of goods sent by the *Guardian*, 1 June 1789, p.115.

9 CO201/4, Clothing sent to N.S.W., 1789, p.148.

10 *Report from the Select Committee on Transportation*, J. Hunter's Evidence, 19.2.1812, HC 1812, p.20.

11 *HRNSW*, Vol. I, Pt. 2, Grenville to Phillip, 24.8.1789, Encl. Phillip's Additional Instructions, 20.8.1789, p.259.

12 J. Campbell, 'Notes on the Early History of the Glebe', *JRAHS*, Vol. XV (1929), Pt. 5, p.298.

13 J. Norris, 'Proposals for Promoting Religion and Literature in Canada, Nova Scotia, and New Brunswick', *The Canadian Historical Review*, Vol. XXXVI (1955), p.335.

14 Quoted in Norris, 'Proposals for Promoting Religion', p.338.

15 *HRNSW*, Vol. VI, Perceval to Bligh, 27.12.1807, p.393.

16 J. Howard, *The State of the Prisons,* London 1929, note 4, p.39.

17 *Twenty-eighth Report from the Select Committee on Finance,* 'Police incl. Convicts, Draft of a Contract between the Lord Commissioners of the Treasury and Jeremy Bentham Esq.', *BSP,* HC 1810, Vol. IV, Appendi F3, p.72.

18 *Report from the Committee Appointed to enquire into the State of H.M.'s Prison in Cold Bath Fields, BSP,* HC 1799, Vol. XXII, Appendix 2, p.74-5.

19 *Report from the Committee on the Laws relating to Penetentiary Houses,* Sir G. Paul's evidence, *BSP,* HC 1811, Vol. III, p.27.

20 E. O'Brien, *The Foundation of Australia,* Sydney 1950, pp.284, 286.

21 *Twenty-eighth Report on Finance, BSP,* HC 1810, Vol. IV, Appendix 0/2, p.122.

22 W. Borrie, *Population Trends and Policies,* Sydney 1948, p.34.

23 *HRA,* Series I, Vol. I, Phillip to Sydney, 11.4.1790, p.166.

24 O'Brien, *Foundation of Australia,* p.178.

25 Ibid., p.14.

26 L. Robson, *The Convict Settlers of Australia,* Melbourne 1965, pp.14-16, 38, 144.

27 Tench, *Sydney's First Four Years,* p.111.

28 *HRNSW,* Vol. II, Extract from Journal of Arthur Bowes, 1788, p.393.

29 D. Collins, *An Account of the English Colony in New South Wales,* Wellington 1910, p.15.

30 *Twenty-eighth Report on Finance,* 'Proposal for a new and less expensive Mode of Employing and Reforming Convicts', Vol. IV, Appendix E, VIII, p.62.

31 *HRNSW,* Vol. I, Pt. 2, Sydney to the Lords Commissioners of the Treasury, 18.8.1786, Encl. Heads of a Plan, p.17.

32 C. Roderick, *First Fleeters: No. 3, 'Parson Richard Johnson',* Australian Broadcasting Commission Talk, 22.4.1963, p.2.

33 R. Johnson Correspondence, Johnson to Fricker, 4.10.1791, n.p. (ML).

34 Ibid., Johnson to Morice, 21.3.1792, n.p.

35 21.3.1792, n.p.

36 Johnson to Sec. SPG, 6.12.1794, n.p.

37 Hassall Correspondence, Vol. II, Marsden to Wilberforce, 1799, p.4 (ML).

38 BT, Box 49, Marsden to Wilberforce, 17.8.1801, p.84 (ML).

39 *HRNSW,* Vol. VII, Wilberforce to Peel, 22.2.1811, p.497.

40 R. Penniman (ed.), *John Locke On Politics And Education,* New York 1947, p.247.

41 Penniman, *John Locke,* p.210.

42 F. Garforth (ed.), *John Locke, Some Thoughts Concerning Education,* London 1964, p.235.

43 *SG,* 12.11.1809.

44 Hassall Correspondence, Vol. II, Marsden to Stokes, 8.10.1814, p.136 (ML).

45 *HRNSW,* Vol. IV, King to Lt. King, 23.5.1800, p.87.

46 Collins, *An Account of the British Colony,* p.366.

47 *HRA,* Series I., Vol. VI, Additional Instructions to Governor Bligh, 20.11.1805, pp.18-19.

48 J. Bonwick, *Australia's First Preacher; the Rev. Richard Johnson,* London n.d. p.51.

Chapter II

1 J. Rousseau, *Émile,* tr. B. Foxley, London 1957, p.56 *passim.*

2 E. Cubberley, *The History of Education,* Cambridge, Mass. 1948, p.536.

3 H. Mathews, *Methodism and the Education of the People 1791-1851,* London 1949, p.20.

4 R. Southey, *The Life of Wesley* (2 vols), Vol. II, London 1925, pp.304-5.

5 N. Curnock, (ed.), *The Journal of Rev. John Wesley, A.M.*, (8 vols), Vol. V, London 1960, pp.352-3.

6 Curnock, *The Journal of Rev. John Wesley*, Vol. III, p.357.

7 Biographical details from D. Pike, (ed.), *Australian Dictionary of Biography 1788-1850*, (2 vols), Melbourne 1966-7, *passim*.

8 G. Mackaness, *Admiral Arthur Phillip*, Sydney 1937, p.3.

9 J. Lawson, *A Town Grammar School Through Six Centuries*, Oxford 1963, p.164 *passim*.

10 V. Goodin, 'Public Education in New South Wales before 1848',

JRAHS, Vol. XXXVI, (1950), Pt. 1, p.2.

11 S. Clark, *The Social Development of Canada*, Toronto 1942, p.178.

12 R. Butts, *A Cultural History of Western Europe*, New York 1955, pp.308-9.

13 *The Works of Jeremy Bentham*, (11 vols), New York 1962, Vol. I, p.349.

14 Wordsworth to Rose (n.d.) quoted in J. Whitney, *Elizabeth Fry*, London 1937, p.164.

15 M. Jones, *The Charity School Movement*, London 1964, p.14.

16 Jones, *The Charity School*, p.22.

17 B. Mandeville, *The Fable of the Bees*, Oxford 1957, p.288 *passim*.

Chapter III

1 Johnson to Morice, 21.3.1792, n.p.

2 Goodin, Pt. 1, p.2.

3 BT, Box 49, Marsden to Archbishop of Canterbury, 2.5.1810, p.292.

4 *SC*, 1812, Richardson's evidence, p.58.

5 Johnson to Sec. SPG, 6.12.1794, n.p.

6 *Great Britain and Ireland Central Criminal Court Session Papers*, 10.1.1787, pp.320 ff.

7 21.3.1792, n.p.

8 Goodin, Pt. 1, p.5.

9 *Session Papers*, 1788-9, 25.2.1789, Case 271, p.322.

10 Quoted in J. Cobley, *Tpe Crimes of the First Fleet Convicts*, Sydney 1970, p.233.

11 Macarthur Papers, Colonel's Company, 1799, n.p. (ML).

12 *SC*, 1812, Richardson, p.56.

13 *HRNSW*, Vol. II, Wilberforce to ——, 2.8.1794, p.247.

14 Collins, p.86.

15 Quoted in Mackaness, *Phillip*, pp.406 f.

16 CO201/45, List of . . . conditional Emanicipations, from 28.9.1800 to 12.8.1806, p.386.

17 W. Connell, 'The Teacher in the Eighteenth and Nineteenth Centuries', *Forum of Education*, Vol. XVI, Nos 2 and 3, October 1957, p.87.

18 P. King, 'Journal of Transactions on Norfolk Island 1791-4', pp.5, 8 (ML).

19 King, 'Transactions', p.215.

20 *Session Papers*, 1789-90, 13.1.1790, Case 189, p.198.

21 Mackaness, *Phillip*, p.350.

22 *HRNSW*, Vol. III, King, Condition of Norfolk Island, 18.10.1796, p.159.

23 *HRNSW*, Vol. III, Marsden to SPG, 2.1.1796, p.1.

24 CO201/1, List of Overseers, 6.7.1796, p.158.

25 BT, Box 49, Extract SPG Journals, p.5.

26 CO201/18, Plan of Sydney, Norfolk Island, 1796, p.165.

27 C. Turney, *The Birth of Education in Australia*, unpublished MEd thesis, University of Sydney, 1960. pp.43-4.

28 Major Joseph Foveaux Letter Book, Norfolk Island, 16.11.1800, p.8 (ML).

29 Ibid.

30 Collins, p.23.

31 R. Border, *Church and State in Australia 1788-1872*, London 1962, p.22.

32 Collins, p.18.

33 Collins, p.188.

34 *HRA*, Series I, Vol. I, Grose to Dundas, 4.9.1793, encl. 1, Johnson to Dundas, 3.9.1793, pp.452-3.

35 Col. Sec., 25.5.1812, 2331, p.140 (NSWSA).

36 CO201/13, List of Public Buildings, 20.8.1796, p.64.

37 *HRA*, Series I, Vol. I, Grose to Dundas, 4.9.1793, p.451.

38 *HRNSW*, Vol. II, Wilberforce to Dundas, 2.8.1794, p.245.

39 *HRNSW*, Vol. II, Johnson to Dundas, 7.8.1794, p.248.

40 *HRNSW*, Vol. II, Newton to Johnson, 4.12.1794, p.273.

41 Convict Indents 1788-1800, AO392 and 4/4003 (ML).

42 Johnson to Sec. SPG 1798, n.p. (ML).

43 Collins, p.381.

44 *HRNSW*, Vol. III, Government and General Order, 3.10.1798, p.495.

45 Johnson to Sec. SPG, 21.9.1799, n.p (ML).

46 *HRNSW*, Vol. II, State of the Settlements at Sydney, Parramatta, and Norfolk Island, 18.3.1792, pp.465-6.

47 *HRNSW*, Vol. I, Pt. 2, Ross to Phillip, 11.2.1791, State of the Settlement, pp.449-50.

48 *HRNSW*, Vol. III, King, Condition of Norfolk Island, 18.10.1796, pp. 154, 160.

49 Mathews, *Methodism and the Education of the People*, p.11.

50 J. Adamson, *English Education 1789-1902*, Cambridge 1964, p.27.

51 *HRA*, Series I, Vol. I, note 241, p.771.

52 Johnson to Sec. SPG, 31.8.1798, extract SPG Journals, p.440 (ML).

Chapter IV

1 *HRNSW*, Vol. I, Pt. 2, Wilberforce to Dundas, 7.8.1792, p.634.

2 CO201/29, N.I. Accounts 1.1.—31.12.1802, p.149 *passim*.

3 Mackaness, *Phillip*, p.376.

4 T. Parsons, 'The Social Composition of the Men of the New South Wales Corps', *JRAHS*, Vol. 50 (June 1964), Pt. IV, p.298.

5 CO201/26, Return of Ninth Company, 27.4.1803, p.58.

6 Bain-Johnson Correspondence, Bain to Seale, 25.11.1789, n.p. (ML).

7 Parsons, 'The Men of the New South Wales Corps', pp.299-300.

8 Ibid., p.302.

9 A. White, *The Story of Army Education 1643-1963*, London 1963, p.18.

10 Ibid.

11 Ibid.

12 Bain-Johnson Correspondence, Bain to SPG, 13.2.1790, n.p.

13 Ibid., Bain from Chatham Barracks, 21.1.1790, n.p.

14 BT, Box 49, Journal of SPG, 15.1.1790, pp.41-2.

15 Johnson to Sec. SPG, 6.12.1794, n.p.

16 Quoted in Turney, p.20.

17 Johnson to SPG, 1.12.1796, extract SPG Journal, p.300 (ML).

18 Johnson to Sec. SPG, 21.9.1799, n.p. (ML).

19 Extract 31.8.1798, SPG Journal, p.440 (ML).

20 21.9.1799, n.p.

21 21.9.1799, n.p.

22 Extract SPG Journals, 11.7.1800, p.143.

23 21.3.1792, n.p.

24 *HRNSW*, Vol. I, Pt. 2, Wilberforce to Dundas, 7.8.1792, p.634.

25 21.3.1792, n.p.

26 BT, Box 88, Return of Lands Granted, 14.3.1795, p.10, and *HRNSW*, Vol. II, Returns of Lands Granted, 13.12.1794-14.3.1795, p.350.

27 21.3.1792, n.p.

28 Johnson to Sec. SPG, 1798, encl. Rules & Articles . . . , 1798, n.p.

29 *SG*, 8.1.1804.

30 *SG*, 23.4.1809.

31 Note on List of . . . conditional Emancipations, No. 58, p.384.

32 J. McGuanne, 'Early Schools of New South Wales', *JRAHS*, Vol. II, Pt. IV (1906-7), p.74.

33 *SG*, 10.11.1805.

34 Memorials, 1810, T. Taber, 29.1.1810, p.303 (NSWSA).

35 BT, Series I, Box 26, Return of Schools 1820, pp.5781.
36 'Transactions', p.215.
37 P. G. King Letter Book, 10.3.1794, p.209 (ML).
38 'Transactions', pp.213 f.
39 *HRNSW*, Vol. IV, King to Hobart, 30.10.1802, p.876.
40 King to Hobart, 30.10.1802, p.876.
41 Digest of Proclamations, G&GO, 10.8.1804 p.595 (NSWSA), and *SG*, 16.8.1804.
42 *HRNSW*, Vol. VI, Present State of H.M.'s Settlements, 12.8.1806, p.152.
43 *HRNSW*, Vol. I, Pt. 2, Rev. T. Walshe to Lord Sydney 1787, pp.119-20.
44 *HRNSW*, Vol. II, Petition from Members of the Roman Catholic Church, 30.11.1792, pp.484-5.
45 *HRNSW*, Vol. IV, Hobart to King, 29.8.1802, pp.826-7.
46 *HRNSW*, Vol. V, Proclamation, 19.4.1803, p.97.
47 *HRA*, Series I, Vol. IV, King to Hobart, 17.9.1803, p.394.
48 *HRNSW*, Vol. V, King to Hobart, 9.5.1803, p.116.
49 Ibid.
50 Quoted in Turney, p.46.
51 *HRNSW*, Vol. VI, King, Present State of H.M.'s Settlements, 12.8.1806, p.152.
52 List of . . . conditional Emancipations, No. 309, p.386.
53 *SG*, 6.10.1805.
54 Goodin, Pt. 2, p.102.
55 BT, Box 49, Marsden to Wilberforce, 27.7.1810, p.88.
56 *HRNSW*, Vol. IV, King to U/S King, 8.11.1801, p.613.
57 G. Mackaness, *The Life of Vice-Admiral Bligh*, Sydney 1951, pp.4-5.
58 CO201/38, An Account of Books Necessary for the Use of Government House at Sydney 18.9.1805, pp.290-1.
59 *HRA*, Series I, Vol. VI, Additional Instructions to Governor Bligh, 20.11.1805, pp.18-19.
60 *HRNSW*, Vol. VI, Castlereagh to Bligh, 31.12.1807, p.400.
61 *HRNSW*, Vol. VII, Hughes to Cowper, 24.1.1810, p.277.
62 *HRNSW*, Vol. VI, Bligh to Piper, 30.12.1806. Encl. General Statement of Inhabitants, 31.12.1806 pp.231-2, and *HRA*, Series I., Vol. VII, Macquarie to Castlereagh, 30.4.1810, encl. 5, General Statement of the Inhabitants, 1.3.1810, pp.280-1.

Chapter V

1 Speech of 27 December 1807, *HRNSW*, Vol. VI, p.393.
2 C. Johnson, *Old-Time Schools and School-Books*, New York 1963, p.2.
3 Quoted in ibid., pp.96-7.
4 Quoted in ibid., p.13.
5 R. Johnson Correspondence, 29.8.1798, Rules . . . , 1798, n.p.
6 *SG*, 12.11.1809.
7 CO201/27, Account of Stationery, 30.12.1802, p.128.
8 McGuanne, p.73.
9 S. Bishop, *Isaac Watts Hymns and Spiritual Songs 1707-1748*, London 1962, pp.XIV-XV.
10 I. Watts, *Divine Songs Attempted in Easy Language for the Use of Children*, London n.d., pp.33-4.
11 F. Darton, *Children's Books in England*, Cambridge 1960, p.111.
12 Quoted in ibid., p.108.
13 Watts, p.16.
14 Ibid., p.40.
15 BT, Series I, Box 20, Return of the First Public School, 31.12.1820, p.3530.
16 *SG*, 9.9.1804.
17 *SG*, 14.10.1804.
18 Bonwick, *Australia's First Preacher*, p.51.
19 Johnson, p.60.
20 G. Mackaness, *Some Letters of Rev. R. Johnson, B.A.*, 2 pts, 1, Sydney 1954, p.7.
21 CO201/33, Estimate of Provisions Received, 20.12.1804, p.235.

22 BT, Box 49, Journal of SPG, Minute of General Meeting, 11.7.1800, p.142.

23 BT, Box 49, Hassall to Burder, 8.8.1801, pp.178-9.

24 BT, Box 49, Hassall to Burder, 28.12.1804, p.240.

25 Marsden Papers, Vol. I, Miss E. Gurney to Marsden, 5.7.1809, pp.75-6.

26 J. Ferguson, *Bibliography of Australia*, Vol. I, Sydney 1941, item 507, p.203.

27 Locke, p.333.

28 T. Dilworth, *The Schoolmaster's Assistant*, London n.d., p.1 *passim*.

29 *SG*, 6.11.1803.

30 *SG*, 13.11.1803.

31 A. Bunker, 'Arithmetic in 1845', *The Australian Mathematics Teacher*, Vol. 20, No. 2 (July 1964), p.43.

32 *SG*, 16.9.1804.

33 *SG*, 31.7.1803.

34 *SG*, 4.3.1804.

35 *SG*, 22.5.1808.

36 *SG*, 4.3.1804.

37 *SG*, 29.7.1804.

38 K. Silber, *Pestalozzi*, London 1965, p.136.

39 J. Pestalozzi, *How Gertrude Teaches Her Children*, London 1966, p.viii.

40 Rules . . . , 1798.

41 *SG*, 8.5.1803.

42 Rules . . . , 1798.

43 *HRNSW*, Vol. III, Johnson to SPG, 1.12.1796, p.184.

44 Locke, pp.265-6.

45 Ibid., p.264.

46 Cubberley, pp.455-6.

47 Johnson, p.43.

48 Mathews, p.59.

Chapter VI

1 BT, Box 27, Marsden to Bigge, 15.3.1821, p.6368.

2 *HRA*, Series I, Vol. I, xxii, and *HRA*, Series I, Vol. I, Second Commission, 2.4.1787, pp.2-7.

3 W. Windeyer, 'Responsible Government', *JRAHS*, Vol. 42 (1957), Pt. 6, note 6, p.309.

4 *HRNSW*, Vol. I, Pt. 2, Commissions of Lieutenant-Governor, Judge-Advocate, Chaplain, and Surgeon, 24.10.1786, pp.26-7.

5 *HRNSW*, Vol. I, Pt. 2, First Year's Civil Salaries 1786, p.33.

6 *HRNSW*, Vol. I, Pt. 2, Instructions, 25.4.1787, p.90.

7 *SG*, 1812, Bligh's evidence, p.36.

8 H. Fulton to Col. Sec., 22.9.1821, LRCS, n.p. (NSWSA).

9 CO201/26, General Standing Order 23.7.1802, p.133.

10 For Marsden's Case *see* BT, Box 3, Marsden to London, 11.3.1821, pp.770 ff., and BT, Box 49, Marsden to Canterbury, 2.5.1810, pp.292 ff.

11 *HRNSW*, Vol. II, Williams to Agents, 27.3.1790, p.757 and note.

12 *HRNSW*, Vol. III, note, p.2.

13 Bonwick, *Australia's First Preacher*, p.37.

14 BT, Biography, Vol. III, Newton to Bull, 27.10.1786, p.757.

15 Quoted in M. Jaeger, *Before Victoria*, London 1967, p.96.

16 Quoted in ibid., p.16.

17 Bonwick, *Australia's First Preacher*, p.63.

18 Ibid., p.64.

19 *HRNSW*, Vol. II, Newton to Johnson, 29.3.1794, p.196.

20 Johnson to Fricker, 4.10.1791, n.p. (ML).

21 Johnson to Fricker, 30.5.1787, n.p.

22 *HRNSW*, Vol. I, Pt. 2, Johnson to Phillip, 23.3.1792, pp.602-3.

23 *HRNSW*, Vol. I, Pt. 2, Johnson to Phillip, 29.2.1792, p.594.

24 Collins, p.282.

25 *HRNSW*, Johnson to Phillip, 29.2.1792, p.594.

26 Johnson to Fricker, 15.11.1788, n.p.

27 *HRNSW*, Vol. II, Johnson to Dundas, 8.4.1794, p.201.

28 *HRNSW*, Vol. II, p.204.

29 *HRNSW*, Vol. II, Grose to Dundas, 5.7.1794, p.238.

30 *HRNSW*, Vol. II, Dundas to Grose, 30.6.1793, p.50.
31 *HRNSW*, Vol. II, Grose to Dundas, 4.9.1793, p.64.
32 *HRNSW*, Vol. II, Palmer to Lindsey, 15.9.1795, p.881.
33 Diary of Rev. S. Marsden 1793, 15.7.1794, n.p. (ML).
34 21.3.1792, n.p.
35 21.3.1792, n.p.
36 *HRNSW*, Vol. II, Wilberforce to Dundas, 2.8.1794, p.245.
37 Extract, SPG Journals, 1.12.1796, p.300 (ML).
38 CO201/26, Return of the Ninth Co., 27.4.1803, p.58.
39 Goodin, Pt. 1, p.10.
40 21.3.1792, n.p.
41 Johnson to Sec. SPG, 6.12.1794, n.p.
42 R. Border, *Church and State in Australia*, p.20.
43 21.3.1792, n.p.
44 W. Armytage, *The German Influence on English Education*, London 1969, p.7.
45 BT, Box 3, Marsden to London, 11.3.1821, p.772.
46 W. Woolls, *A Short Account of the Character and Labours of the Rev. S. Marsden*, Parramatta n.p., p.7.
47 J. Bonwick, *Curious Facts of Old Colonial Days*, London 1870, p.19.
48 Hassall Correspondence, Vol. II, Marsden to Stokes, 26.10.1795, p.21.
49 Hassall Correspondence, Vol. II, Marsden to Stokes, 1804, p.85.
50 Hassall Correspondence, Vol. II, Marsden to Stokes, 27.3.1817, p.153.
51 Marsden to London, 11.3.1821, pp.774-5.
52 *HRNSW*, Vol. V, King to Banks, 14.8.1804, p.450.
53 *HRNSW*, Vol. V, Return of the number of acres of land sown, 14.8.1804, pp.432-3.
54 R. Bell, 'Samuel Marsden—Pioneer Pastoralist', *JRAHS*, Vol. 56, Pt. I (March 1970), p.53.
55 Biographical note by A. Yarwood, *ADB*, II, p.208.
56 S. Johnstone, *Samuel Marsden*, Sydney 1932, p.33.
57 BT, Box 3, Encl. Marsden to London, 11.3.1821, extract Marsden to Bigge, *c.* 1820, pp.778-9.
58 Hassall Correspondence, Vol. II, Marsden to Stokes, 26.11.1816, p.111.
59 S. Marsden, *A Few Observations on the Toleration of the Catholic Religion in N. South Wales*, n.d., n.p., (ML).
60 Quoted in J. Marsden, in *Life and Work of Samuel Marsden*, Wellington 1913, p.53.
61 Marsden, *A Few Observations*, n.p.
62 Ibid.
63 Ibid.
64 J. King, *Ten Decades—The Australian Centenary Story of the London Missionary Society*, London, n.d., p.49.
65 Ibid., p.47.
66 J. Bigge, *Report into the Colony of New South Wales*, 3 vols, HC, 1822-3, III, p.76.
67 BT, Box 15, Marsden to Smith, 10.1.1817, p.1624.
68 Jones, *Charity School Movement*, p.153.
69 BT, Box 26, Bigge to Marsden, 20.1.1821, extract, p.5801. For a fuller discussion *see* Chapter IX.
70 BT, Box 52, Marsden to Pratt, 1.4.1822, p.1105.
71 BT, Box 26, Eyre to Bigge, 3.2.1821, pp.6132-3.
72 Rev. M. Atkinson to Marsden, 31.7.1802, Marsden Papers, Vol. 9, p.1.
73 BT, Box 26, Marsden, Observations on Mr Eagar's evidence, 3.2.1821, p.6130.
74 Hassall Correspondence, Vol. II, Marsden to Stokes, 24.8.1801, p.57.
75 Johnstone, *Marsden*, p.38.
76 Bonwick, *Curious Facts*, p.26.
77 Hassall Correspondence, Vol. II, Marsden to Stokes, 29.3.1817, p.154.
78 BT, Box 49, Hassall to Burder, 8.8.1801, p.177.
79 Marsden Papers, Vol. 9, Letter of Appreciation of 1807, pp.5-10.
80 BT, Box 16, Marsden to Hosking and Bowden, 24.11.1817, p.2021.
81 Goulburn to Hill, 26.7.1822, LSCS, p.82 (NSWSA).

Chapter VII

1 Hassall Correspondence, Vol. I, Directors LMS to Missionaries 1799, pp.24-5.
2 J. Morison, *The Fathers and Founders of the London Missionary Society*, London n.d., p.ix.
3 W. Brown, *History of the Propagation of Christianity Among The Heathen Since The Reformation* (3 vols), Vol. II, London n.d., p.99.
4 W. Gunson, *Evangelical Missionaries in the South Seas 1797-1860*, unpublished PhD thesis, Australian National University, 1959, p.421.
5 Gunson, *Evangelical Missionaries*, p.19.
6 J. Wilson, *A Missionary Voyage to the Southern Pacific Ocean*, London 1966, p.416.
7 A Sermon and Charge, delivered at Sion-Chapel, 28.7.1796, p.vii (ML).
8 Quoted in Gunson, p.63.
9 Wilson, pp.5-6, and *ADB*, Vol. I, pp.251-3, and Haweis Papers, Harper, 'A Missionary Journal', 10.8.1796, pp.299-300 (ML).
10 Wilson, p.4.
11 J. Jorgensen, *State of Christianity in the Island of Otaheite*, London 1811, p.98.
12 Gunson, p.124.
13 Ibid., pp.408-9.
14 Quoted in A. Moorehead, *The Fatal Impact*, London 1966, p.70.
15 Ibid., pp.83-4.
16 Wilson, pp.141-2.
17 Brown, II, pp.108, 141.
18 J. Ellis, *Life of William Ellis*, London 1873, p.xix.
19 Brown, II, p.134.
20 *HRNSW*, Vol. III, LMS to Hunter, October 1799, p.731.
21 *HRNSW*, Vol. III, Henry to LMS, 29.8.1799, p.712.
22 *HRNSW*, Vol. III, LMS to Missionaries, *c.* 1799, p.732.
23 *SC*, 1812, Bligh's evidence, p.37.
24 Hassall Correspondence, Vol. I, Directors LMS to Missionaries, *c.* 1799, p.24.

25 Quoted in W. Connell, 'The Teacher in the Eighteenth and Nineteenth Centuries', p.86.
26 BT, Box 49, Crook to Sec., 18.6.1813, p.329.
27 BT, Series I, Box 27, Proceedings Taken at the Court of Parramatta, 5.8.1821, p.6435.
28 Quoted in D. Smart, *The Role of the Methodist Church in New South Wales Education in 1880*, unpublished MEd thesis, University of Sydney, 1967, p.40.
29 Col. Sec. to Missionaries, 22.2.1810, Miscellaneous Persons, p.94 (NSWSA).
30 BT, Box 49, Missionaries to LMS, 25.8.1799, p.101.
31 *HRNSW*, Vol. III, Henry to LMS, 29.8.1799, pp.714-5.
32 BT, Box 49, p.101.
33 *HRNSW*, Vol. IV, Hassall to LMS, 22.4.1800, p.75.
34 BT, Box 49, Hassall to Directors, 14.10.1800, p.153.
35 BT, Box 49, Hassall to Society, 29.9.1800, pp.145-6.
36 BT, Box 49, Hassall to Burder, 8.8.1801, p.178.
37 BT, Box 49, Hassall, 29.9.1800, p.146.
38 *HRNSW*, Vol. III, Missionaries to Directors, 25.8.1799, p.708.
39 *HRNSW*, Vol. IV, Hassall to LMS, 29.9.1800, p.210.
40 List of ... conditional Emancipations, No. 81, p.384.
41 Goodin, Pt. 4, Appendix III, p.208.
42 Foveaux, p.8.
43 BT, Box 49, Harris to ——, 26.7.1805, p.252.
44 *SG*, 26.8.1804.
45 BT, Box 49, Harris, 26.7.1805, p.253.
46 Wilson, p.5.
47 Ibid., p.142.
48 J. Ham, *Life of W. Crook*, Melbourne 1846, p.12.
49 *HRNSW*, Vol. V, Crook to Hardcastle, 8.11.1803, p.257.

50 *HRNSW*, Vol. V, Crook to ——, Parramatta 1804, p.538.
51 Ibid., p.537.
52 BT, Box 49, Crook to LMS, Parramatta 1804, p.219.
53 Crook, 1804, p.537.
54 Ibid., p.537.
55 *SG*, 19.8.1804.
56 *SG*, 9.6.1805.
57 *SG*, 22.5.1808.
58 BT, Box 49, Crook to Secretary, 18.6.1813, p.329.
59 Biographical note by Gunson, *ADB*, I, p.260.
60 J. King, *Ten Decades*, p.47.
61 BT, Box 49, Crook to Secretary, 18.6.1813, p.329.
62 R. Arndell, 'Ebenezer', *The N.S.W.*

Presbyterian (4 parts), Pt. 1 (1964), p.9.
63 CO201/20, James Mein, 7.9.1801, p.282.
64 Arndell, 15.5.1964, Pt III, p.9.
65 Hassall Correspondence, Vol. I, Hassall to Hardcastle, 5.11.1808, pp.259, 261.
66 Arndell, 29.5.1964, Pt. IV, p.11.
67 Ibid.
68 Quoted in Arndell, Pt. III, p.9.
69 Bigge, III, p.76.
70 *SG*, Philo Free, 4.1.1817.
71 *ADB*, I, pp.251-3, 521, 365, and Wilson, pp.5-6, and Haweis Papers, p.300.
72 *HRNSW*, Vol. V, King to Hobart, 1.3.1804, p.324.

Chapter VIII

1 CO201/18, King to Portland, 16.1.1797, encl. 7, N.I. Settlers to King n.d., p.140.
2 W. Tench, p.16.
3 *HRNSW*, Vol. II, Journal of Lt. King, June 1787, pp.517-8.
4 S. Curtis, *History of Education in Great Britain*, London 1965, p.111.
5 *Report from the Committee Appointed to Review and Consider the Several Laws which Concern the Relief and Settlement of the Poor . . .* , MDCCLXXV, and *Report from the Committee Appointed to Make Enquiries Relating to the Employment, Relief, and Maintenance of Vagrants . . .* , MDCCLXXVI, *BSP*, Vol. IV, HC, 1775-6 *passim*.
6 Quoted in K. de Schweinitz, *England's Road to Social Security*, London 1943, p.61.
7 W. Stewart and W. McCann, *The Educational Innovators*, I., London 1967, pp.63-5.
8 S. Clark, *Social Development of Canada*, p.99.
9 Cubberley, p.813.
10 Johnson to Sec. SPG, 6.12.1794, n.p.
11 A Statement of the Married and Unmarried Women, 12.8.1806, Banks Papers, Vol. 22, p.13 (ML).
12 Collins, p.45.

13 CO201/9, Proclamation, 29.12.1791, pp.60-1.
14 *HRNSW*, Vol. III, King, Condition of Norfolk Island, 8.10.1796, p.160.
15 BT, Box 49, Minute of General Meeting, 19.6.1801, p.174.
16 P. King, Letter Book 1797-1806, 19.12.1800, p.171.
17 King, Letter Book, p.171.
18 Major J. Foveaux, Letter Book, 12.10.1801, p.30.
19 *HRNSW*, Vol. III, Johnson to Sec. SPG, 1.12.1796, p.184.
20 Hassall Correspondence, Vol. II, Marsden to Wilberforce, Parramatta 1799, 6.2.1800, pp.4, 7.
21 G. Abbott, 'Government Works and Services' in G. Abbott and N. Nairn (eds), *Economic Growth of Australia 1788-1821*, Melbourne 1969, p.312.
22 Collins, p.366.
23 *HRNSW*, Vol. III, Johnson, 1.12.1796, p.184.
24 Collins, p.366.
25 *HRNSW*, Vol. IV, Orphan Asylum, 11.10.1800, p.233.
26 Hassall Correspondence, Vol. II, Marsden to Wilberforce, 6.2.1800, p.11.
27 *SC*, 1812, Hunter, p.22.

28 *HRNSW*, Vol. IV, King to Johnson, 7.8.1800, p.135.
29 Mrs. E. Paterson to Capt. Johnson, 3.10.1800, pp.3-4 (ML).
30 Hassall Correspondence, Vol. II, Marsden to Stokes, 8.10.1814, p.136.
31 Hassall Correspondence, Vol. II, 6.2.1800, p.11.
32 *HRNSW*, Vol. IV, Orphan House Committee, 15.9.1800, p.138.
33 *HRNSW*, Vol. IV, Orphan Asylum, 11.10.1800, p.233.
34 BT, Box 49, Hassall to Burder, 17.8.1801, p.185.
35 *HRNSW*, Vol. IV, Kent to Banks, 6.12.1801, p.631.
36 *HRNSW*, Vol. IV, Orphan Asylum, 11.10.1800, p.232.
37 CO201/25, Proceedings of the Committee, 24.3.1803, p.204.
38 M. Bassett, *The Governor's Lady*, Melbourne 1961, p.65.
39 *HRNSW*, Vol. IV, Proceedings of a Committee, 8.9.1800, p.137.
40 *HRNSW*, Vol. IV, Orphan House Committee, 15.9.1800, p.138.
41 *SC*, 1812, Bligh's Evidence, p.40, and CO201/25, Proceedings of the Committee, 1.6.1804, p.206.
42 *HRNSW*, Vol. IV, Hassall to Burder, 8.8.1801, p.447.
43 BT, Box 24, Orphan School Report, 22.8.1820, p.4913.
44 BT, Box 49, Hassall to Burder, 17.8.1801, pp.183-4.
45 Hassall to Burder, 17.8.1801, p
46 Hassall Correspondence, Vol. Marsden to Mrs. Stokes, 24.8.1 p.54.
47 *SG*, 23.10.1808.
48 Hassall Correspondence, Vol. Marsden to Wilberforce, 27.7.180 p.23.
49 *HRNSW*, Vol. VI, Present State of H.M.'s Settlements, 12.8.1806, p.152.
50 Bigge, III, p.71.
51 *HRNSW*, Vol. V, King to Hobart, 14.8.1804, p.429.
52 J. Cleverley, *The Administration of State-Assisted Elementary Education in Mainland New South Wales 1789-1855*, unpublished PhD thesis,

University of Sydney, 1967, pp.43-4, and CO201/41, CO201/25, CO201/ 36 *passim*, and *SG*, 1805 *passim*.
53 CO201/25, Proceedings of the Committee, 3.10.1802, p.202.
54 CO201/25, Treasurer to Baudin, 5.10.1802, p.203.
55 *HRNSW*, Vol. IV, Orphan Asylum, 11.10.1800, p.233.
56 CO201/25, Proceedings of the Committee, n.d. p.202.
57 BT, Series I, Box 12, King to Commissary, 16.6.1806, p.132.
58 *HRNSW*, Vol. IV, King to Hobart, 30.10.1802, p.869.
59 *SG*, 5.10.1806.
60 CO201/40, Statement of Receipts and Disbursements, 1.1.1806-12.8.1806, p.3.
61 BT, Series I, Box 12, Marsden to King, 25.1.1805, pp.123-4.
62 BT, Series I, Box 12, Orphan School Committee to Marsden, 26.6.1806, p.135.
63 BT, Series I, Box 12, King to Commissary, 7.7.1806, pp.140-1.
64 BT, Box 26, Marsden to Bigge, 30.1.1821, p.6039.
65 BT, Box 49, Marsden to Wilberforce, 17.8.1810, p.82.
66 Marsden Papers, Vol. 9, Atkinson to Marsden, 31.7.1802, p.1.
67 BT, Box 49, Minute of General 19.6.1801, p.173.
68 ., Trustees of the Orphan n, 1.7.1807, p.300.
69 Proceedings of the Com-, p.202.
70 3.1810, 4/1723, p.208 iscellaneous Papers re School Committee, Campbell to Committee, 21.6.1817, n.p. (NSWSA).
71 Miscellaneous Papers re Orphan School Committee, Campbell to Committee, 21.6.1817, n.p.
72 *HRNSW*, Vol. IV, Portland to King, 19.6.1801, p.424.
73 CO201/25, Proceedings of the Committee, 17.4.1802, p.200.
74 Liverpool to Macquarie, 5.5.1812, 4/1616, p.156 (NSWSA).

75 Biographical note by J. Byrnes, *ADB*, I, p.563.
76 CO201/32, Proceedings of the Committee, 27.5.1803, p.101.
77 CO201/25, Proceedings of the Committee, 10.8.1802, p.201.
78 J. Harris to Mrs. King, 25.10.1807, King Papers, Vol. 8, pp.246-7.
79 Harris, 25.10.1807, p.247.
80 BT, Box 49, Marsden to Wilberforce, 17.8.1801, p.83.
81 BT, Box 49, Crook to Sec., 5.5.1805, p.250.
82 BT, Box 49, Crook to LMS, 18.6.1813, p.327.
83 *SG*, 24.11.1805.
84 *SC*, 1812, Bligh, p.40.
85 *HRNSW*, Vol. VI, Bligh to Windham, 7.2.1807, p.251.
86 *HRNSW*, Vol. VII, Brown to Castlereagh, 13.10.1809, p.217.
87 BT, Box 49, Crook to LMS, 18.6.1813, p.327.
88 BT, Box 49, Marsden to Arch-

bishop of Canterbury, 2.5.1810, p.291.
89 *SC*, 1812, p.39.
90 BT, Box 12, The Committee of the Orphan Institution, pp.328-331.
91 C. Reeves, *A History of Tasmanian Education*, Melbourne 1935, p.4.
92 Extract, Shee to Harrison, 7.1.1811, 4/1616, p.88 (NSWSA).
93 D. Mann, *The Present Picture of New South Wales*, London 1811, p.35.
94 CO201/25, Proceedings of the Committee, 24.3.1803, p.204.
95 *SC*, 1812, p.40.
96 CO201/40, Statement of Receipts of Disbursements, 1.1.1806-12.8.1806, p.3.
97 CO201/44, Trustees of the Orphan Institution, 1.7.1807, p.300.
98 CO201/32, Proceedings of the Committee, 24.9.1803, p.101.
99 Goodin, III, p.133.
100 BT, Box 27, BA, Marsden to Bigge, 15.3.1821, p.6367.
101 *SG*, 1.1.1824.

Chapter IX

1 P. Cunningham, *Two Years in New South Wales* (2 vols), Vol. II, London 1827, p.46.
2 B. Smith, *European Vision and the South Pacific 1768-1850*, Oxford 1960, p.126.
3 BT, Box 13, G&GO, 10.12.1814, p.916.
4 Collins, p.324.
5 Ibid., pp.97 ff.
6 Ibid., p.258.
7 Ibid., pp.355, 366.
8 Ibid., p.53.
9 *SG*, 8.9.1821.
10 J. Hunter, *An Historical Journal of Events at Sydney and at Sea*, J. Bach (ed.), Sydney 1968, p.314.
11 Johnson to Fricker, 9.4.1790, n.p.
12 Hunter, *Historical Journal*, p.275.
13 Collins, p.342.
14 Hunter, p.359.
15 Collins, p.349.
16 21.3.1792, n.p.
17 Hassall Correspondence, Vol. II,

E. Marsden to Stokes, 1.5.1796, p.26.
18 J. Marsden, *Memoirs of the Life and Labours of the Rev. Samuel Marsden*, London 1858, p.84.
19 BT, Box 20, Marsden to Bigge, *c.* 1820, pp.3498-9.
20 *SG*, 8.9.1821.
21 J. Dredge, *Brief Notices of the Aborigines of New South Wales*, Geelong 1845, pp.11-12.
22 *HRNSW*, Vol. III, Missionary Directors to Hunter, October 1799, extract LMS to Missionaries, n.d., p.732.
23 BT, Box 49, Henry to LMS, 29.8.1799, pp.113-4.
24 Biographical note by Gunson, *ADB*, I, p.252.
25 Gunson, *ADB*, II, p.438-9.
26 BT, Box 49, Shelley to Burder, 6.10.1814, pp.380-1.
27 *HRA*, Series I, Vol. VIII, Macquarie to Bathurst, 8.10.1814, p.368.

28 Collins, p.242.

29 *HRA*, Series I, Vol. VIII, Macquarie to Bathurst, 8.10.1814, encl. 1, Shelley to Macquarie, 8.4.1814, p.371.

30 *HRA*, Series I, Vol. VIII, encl. 4, Macquarie to Bathurst, 8.10.1814, p.373.

31 Cleverley, p.97.

32 *HRA*, Series I, Vol. VIII, Macquarie to Bathurst, 8.10.1814, encl. 1, Shelley to Macquarie, 8.4.1814, p.370.

33 G&GO, 10.12.1814, p.917.

34 *HRA*, Series I, Vol. VIII, Macquarie to Bathurst, 24.3.1815, p.467.

35 Miscellaneous Papers re Black Native Institution, Vouchers, 1814-23, Native Estimate, 28.12.1816, n.p. (NSWSA).

36 BT, Box 26, Bigge to Marsden, 20.1.1821, extract, p.5801.

37 Marsden to Committee of Native Institution, 12.12.1821, 4/1752, pp.11-12 (NSWSA).

38 BT, Box 20, Marsden to Commissioner of Enquiry, *c.* 1820, pp.3499-500.

39 *HRA*, Series I, Vol. VIII, Macquarie to Bathurst, 24.3.1815, p.467.

40 BT, Box 50, Shelley to Burder, 30.6.1815, p.203.

41 Macquarie's Diary, 1816-18, 6.12.1816, p.22.

42 BT, Box 50, 'Names of the Children of the Aborigines received into the Native Institution Parramatta, since . . . 10.1.1814', p.480.

43 BT, Box 50, 'Names of the Children . . .', p.480.

44 B. Bridges, 'Aboriginal Education in Eastern Australia (N.S.W.) 1788-1855', *Australian Journal of Education*, Vol. 12, No. 3 (October 1968), p.231.

45 *SG*, 17.4.1819.

46 *HRA*, Series I, Vol. X, Macquarie to Bathurst, 27.7.1822, p.677.

47 Bigge, III, p.73 ff.

48 *HRA*, Series I, Vol. X, Macquarie to Bathurst, 27.7.1822, p.677.

49 BT, Box 52, Hill to London, 6.3.1822, p.1099.

50 *Report from the Committee on the Aborigines' Question*, 1838, Mrs. Shelley's evidence, 25.9.1838. *V & P.NSWLC*, 1838, p.55.

51 *HRA*, Series I, Vol. X, Macquarie to Bathurst, 24.2.1820, encl. 1, Cartwright to Macquarie, 6.12.1819, p.264.

52 *HRA*, Series I, Vol. X, Macquarie to Bathurst, 24.2.1820, p.263.

53 BT, Box 52, Marsden to Pratt, 15.1.1823, p.1228.

54 BT, Box 54, Extracts from the Report of the CMS Committee, 4.5.1824, pp.1817-8.

55 *SG*, 1.1.1824.

56 *HRA*, Series I, Vol. XI, Brisbane to Bathurst, 3.10.1825, p.864.

57 *HRA*, Series I, Vol. XIV, Darling to Huskisson, 27.3.1828, encl. Scott to Darling, 1.8.1827, p.56.

58 Scott Thomas Hobbes, Archdeacon, Letter Book, I, Scott to Hall, 6.2.1827, pp.357-8 (ML).

59 Stock Returns and Related Correspondence, n.p. (NSWSA).

60 Blacktown Correspondence and Stock Returns, Hall to Archdeacon Scott, 26.7.1828, n.p.

61 Stock Returns, 20.4.1829, n.p.

62 Quoted in Bridges, 'Aboriginal Education in Eastern Australia', p.232.

63 Ibid.

64 *HRA*, Series I, Vol. XIV, Darling to Murray, 2.1.1829, encl. 2, Hall to Murray, 26.11.1828, p.597.

65 *HRA*, Series I, Vol. VIII, Bathurst to Macquarie, 4.12.1815, p.645.

66 *HRA*, Series I, Vol. XIII, pp.433-4.

67 *HRA*, Series I, Vol. XIV, Darling to Huskisson, 27.3.1828, encl. 1, Scott to Darling, 1.8.1827, pp.62-3.

68 Collins, p.349.

69 Tench, pp.221-2.

70 Rev. T.F. Palmer, Letter from Sydney, 13.6.1795, J. Ferguson, *Bibliography of Australia*, p.88.

71 *HRNSW*, Vol. IV, Proclamation, 30.6.1802, p.795.

72 Quoted in A. Price, *White Settlers and Native Peoples*, Melbourne 1950, p.107.

73 J. McCulloch, *A Dictionary, Geographical, Statistical, and Historical* (2 vols), Vol. I, London 1854, p.230.
74 Hunter, p.275.

75 D. Mulvaney, 'The Australian Aborigines 1606-1929 . . .' (2 parts), *HSANZ*, Vol. 8, No. 30 (May 1958), Part I, p.145.
76 McCulloch, *Dictionary*, p.229 *passim*.

Chapter X

1 *SC*, 1812, p.35.
2 Banks Papers, Vol. 6, Marsden to Mrs. Cook, n.d., quoted Fulton, *c.* 1809, p.160 (ML).
3 Quoted in D. Hainsworth, (ed.), *Builders and Adventurers*, Melbourne 1968, p.13.
4 Hassall Correspondence, Vol. II, E. Marsden to Stokes, 6.9.1799, pp.37-8.
5 Mrs. Macarthur to Miss Kingdon, 1.9.1795, quoted in S. Macarthur Onslow (ed.), *Some Early Records of the Macarthurs of Camden*, Sydney 1914, pp.46-7.
6 Bassett, pp.115 *passim*.
7 Note by M.H. Ellis, *JRAHS*, Newsletter, July 1968, p.6.
8 Macarthur, *Early Records*, p.101.
9 *SG*, 4.1.1807.
10 Quoted in Arndell, *Ebenezer*, III, 15.5.1964, p.9.
11 Biographical note by A. Fink, *ADB*, II, p.552.
12 *Report from the Select Committee on Transportation*, 1837 (2 vols), J. Mudie's evidence, 5.5.1837, HC, II, 1837, p.102.
13 C. Rowcroft, *Tales of the Colonies*, London 1850, p.519.
14 H. Kingsley, *Geoffrey Hamlyn*, Melbourne 1952, p.175.
15 L. Robson, 'The Origin of Women Convicts Sent to Australia 1787-1852', *HSANZ*, Vol. II, No. 41 (November 1963), p.52.
16 *Sydney Morning Herald*, 23.9.1851.
17 *SG*, Indexes, 1804-9.
18 Locke, p.281.
19 W. Medlin, *The History of Educational Ideas in the West*, New York 1967, p.108.
20 Curtis, *History of Education in Great Britain*, p.125.
21 *SG*, 19.8.1804.

22 *SG*, 23.12.1804.
23 *SG*, 9.11.1806.
24 *SG*, 19.8.1804.
25 Goodin, Pt. 2, p.86.
26 *SG*, 6.11.1803.
27 L. Murray, *English Grammar*, York 1824, pp.335-7.
28 Ibid., pp.341-7.
29 Johnson, p.365.
30 Quoted in Darton, p.3.
31 CO201/7, Account of Stores, 16.12.1792, p.399.
32 *HRNSW*, Vol. V, Crook to ——, 1804, p.538.
33 *SG*, 22.5.1808.
34 *SG*, 29.7.1804.
35 *SG*, 19.8.1804.
36 Darton, p.54.
37 Ibid., p.164.
38 Ibid., pp.96-7.
39 Quoted in J. Kamm, *Hope Deferred*, London 1965, p.132.
40 Quoted in D. Gardiner, *English Girlhood at School*, Oxford 1929, p. 440.
41 Quoted in Kamm, pp.112, 114.
42 *SC*, 1812, p.12.
43 *SG*, 16.8.1807.
44 *SG*, 10.8.1806.
45 *SG*, 16.8.1807.
46 *SG*, 26.3.1809.
47 *SG*, 10.8.1806.
48 CO201/48, Marchant to Sec. of State, 27.2.1808, p.61.
49 CO201/48, Coe to Banks, 5.3.1808, p.75.
50 *SG*, 6.1.1805.
51 *SC*, 1812, p.22.
52 *SC*, 1812, p.37.
53 *SG*, 31.7.1803.
54 *SG*, 8.5.1803.
55 *SG*, 8.5.1803.
56 *HRA*, Series I, Vol. XV, Darling to Murray, 18.10.1829, encl. Scott to Darling, 1.9.1829, pp.220-1.

57 Mrs. Molley to H. Story, January 1835, quoted in A. Hasluck, *Portrait with a Background*, Melbourne 1966, p.132.

58 J. Ross, *A Voyage of Discovery and Research in the Southern and Antarctic Regions 1839-1843* (2 vols), London 1847, Vol. I, p.120.

Chapter XI

1 Hassall Correspondence, Vol. II, Marsden to Stokes, 4.6.1819, p.179.
2 Cubberley, p.560.
3 Quoted in C. Cipolla, *Literacy and Development in the West*, London 1969, p.65.
4 Ibid.
5 *HRNSW*, Vol. IV, King to Johnson, 7.8.1800, p.135, and *HRNSW*, VI, Bligh to Piper, 30.12.1806, encl. General Statement of Inhabitants, 31.12.1806, pp.231-2.
6 Reeves, *History of Tasmanian Education*, p.2.
7 K. Robinson, 'Population and Land Use in the Sydney District: 1788-1820', *New Zealand Geographer*, IX (1953), pp.147-8.
8 T. Perry, *Australia's First Frontier*, Melbourne 1965, p.21.
9 Macarthur Onslow, p.47.
10 Goodin, IV, Appendix II, pp.205-6.
11 Cipolla, p.102.
12 Cubberley, note 1, p.627.
13 A. Bell, *An Analysis of the Experiment in Education Made at Egmore, Near Madras*, London 1807, p.v.
14 Ibid., pp.81-2.
15 Bigge, III, p.75.
16 Details in Goodin, Pt. 4, Appendix I, pp.204-5.
17 Bigge, I, p.105.
18 Cunningham, *Two Years in New South Wales*, Vol. II, pp.47, 49.
19 Quoted in K. Macnab and R. Ward, 'The Nature and Nurture of the First Generation of Native-born Australians', *HSANZ*, Vol. 10, No. 39 (November 1962), p.305.

20 W. Hughes, *The Australian Colonies*, London, 1852, p.113.
21 Macnab and Ward, 'Nature and Nurture', p.301.
22 Quoted in Macnab and Ward, p.302.
23 Hughes, *The Australian Colonies*, p.114.
24 A. Gilchrist, *John Dunmore Lang* (2 vols), Melbourne 1951, Vol. I, p.135.
25 W. Woolls, *Miscellanies in Prose and Verse*, Sydney 1838, p.84.
26 Ibid., p.91.
27 Ibid., p.96.
28 Macnab and Ward, pp.292, 296.
29 Hassall Correspondence, Vol. II, Marsden to Stokes, 14.3.1816, p.142.
30 A Statement of the Married and Unmarried Woman, 12.8.1806, p.13.
31 CO201/45, Marsden to Cooke, 21.11.1807, pp.320 ff.
32 *HRNSW*, Vol. V, Wilberforce to Castlereagh, 9.11.1805, p.727.
33 Rowland Hassall Papers, Marsden to Hassall, 30.3.1808, p.187, and 7.6.1808, p.194.
34 BT, Box 49, Marsden to Canterbury, 2.5.1810, p.292.
35 *SG*, 29.10.1809.
36 Note on memorial of W. Baker, 23.12.1816, 4/1736, p.8 (NSWSA).
37 *HRA*, Series I, Vol. VIII, Macquarie to Bathurst, 7.10.1814, p.297.
38 *SG*, 25.3.1820.
39 H. Parkes, 'The Public Estate', in a collection of unpublished papers in proof, Sydney 1882, p.1 (ML).

SELECT BIBLIOGRAPHY

This bibliography is arranged according to the following classification:

A. Manuscript material

B. Printed material

    1. Official and semi-official documents

    2. Books and pamphlets

    3. Articles

    4. Newspapers

C. Unpublished theses

A. *Manuscript material*

Bain-Johnson Correspondence (ML).

Banks Papers (ML).

Bonwick Transcripts including Bigge Appendix, Missionary and Biography (ML).

Colonial Office 201/1-50 (PRO).

Convict Indents (NSWSA).

Digest of Proclamations (NSWSA).

Foveaux Letter Book (ML).

Governors' Dispatches (NSWSA).

Hassall Correspondence (ML).

Haweis Papers (ML).

Johnson Correspondence (ML).

Journal of SPG (ML).

King Papers (ML).

Letters Received Colonial Secretary (NSWSA).

Letters Sent Colonial Secretary (NSWSA).

Macarthur Papers (ML).

Marsden, S., *A few observations on the toleration of the Catholic religion in N. South Wales* (NSWSA).

Marsden Correspondence (ML)

Memorials to the Governor (NSWSA).

Miscellaneous Persons Letters Colonial Secretary (NSWSA).

Miscellaneous Papers re Black Native Institution (NSWSA).

Scott (Archdeacon T.H.) Letterbook (ML)

Stock Returns and Related Correspondence (NSWSA).

Summary of Records (NSWSA).

B. *Printed material*

1. OFFICIAL AND SEMI-OFFICIAL DOCUMENTS

Great Britain and Ireland Central Criminal Court Session Papers, 1787-90.

Historical Records of Australia, 33 vols. in 4 series, Library Committee of Commonwealth Parliament 1914-25.

Historical Records of New South Wales, 7 vols., Government Printer, Sydney, 1893-1901.

Report from the Committee Appointed to Make Enquiries Relating to the Employment, Relief, and Maintenance, of Vagrants ..., HC, MDCCLXXVI.

Report from the Committee Appointed to Review and Consider the several Laws which concern the Relief and Settlement of the Poor . . ., HC, MDCCLXXV.

Report from the Committee Appointed on the Laws relating to Penetentiary Houses, HC, 1811.

Report from the Committee on the Aborigines' Question, V&P NSW, LC, 1838.

Report from the Select Committee on Transportation, HC, 1812.

Report from the Select Committee on Transportation, HC, 1837.

Report of the Commissioner of Inquiry into the Colony of New South Wales, 3 vols., HC, 1822-3.

Report from the Committee Appointed to Enquire into the State of H.M.'s Prison in Cold Bath Fields, HC, 1799.

Twenty-eighth Report from the Select Committee on Finance, HC, 1810.

2. BOOKS AND PAMPHLETS

Abbott, G., and Nairn, N., (eds.), *Economic Growth of Australia,1788-1821*, Melbourne University Press, 1969.

Adamson, J., *English Education 1789-1902*, Cambridge University Press, 1964.

Armytage, W., *Four Hundred Years of English Education*, Cambridge University Press, 1964.

Austin, A. G., *Australian Education 1799-1800: Church, State and Public Education in Colonial Australia*, 2nd edn, Pitman, Melbourne 1965.

Bassett, M., *The Governor's Lady*, Melbourne University Press, 1961.

Bell, A., *An Analysis of the Experiment in Education Made at Egmore, Near Madras*, 3rd edn, Cadell and Davies, London 1807.

Bentham, J., *The Works of Jeremy Bentham*, 11 vols, Russell and Russell, New York 1962.

Bonwick, J., *Australia's First Preacher; the Rev. Richard Johnson*, Sampson, Low, Marston, London 1898.

——, *Curious Facts of Old Colonial Days*, Sampson, Low, Son & Marston, London 1870.

Border, R., *Church and State in Australia 1788-1872*, SPCK, London 1962.

Bowen, J., (introd.), J.A. Comenius, *Orbis Sensualium Pictus*, Sydney University Press, 1967.

Broudy, H., and Palmer, J., *Exemplars of Teaching Method*, McNally, Chicago 1965.

Brown, W., *History of the Propagation of Christianity Among the Heathen Since the Reformation*, 3 vols, David Brown and others, Edinburgh n.d.

Butts, R. F., *A Cultural History of Western Education*, 2nd edn, McGraw-Hill, New York 1955.

Cipolla, C., *Literacy and Development in the West*, Penguin Books, Harmondsworth 1969.

Clark, S., *The Social Development of Canada*, University of Toronto Press, 1942.

Cobley, J., *Sydney Cove 1788*, Hodder and Stoughton, London 1963.

Cole, P., *A History of Educational Thought*, Oxford University Press, London 1931.

Collins, D., *An Account of the English Colony in New South Wales*, Whitcomb and Tombs, Wellington 1910.

Cubberley, E., *The History of Education*, Constable, London 1948.

Cunningham, P., *Two Years in New South Wales*, 2 vols, 3rd edn, H. Colburn, London 1828.

Curnock, N., (ed.), *The Journal of Rev. John Wesley, A.M.*, 8 vols, Epworth Press, London 1960.

Curtis, S. J., *History of Education in Great Britain*, University Tutorial Press, London 1963.

Darton, F. J. Harvey, *Children's Books in England*, 2nd edn, Cambridge University Press, 1960.

Dilworth, T., *The Schoolmaster's Assistant*, A. Millar and others, York 1791.

Ferguson, J. A., *Bibliography of Australia*, Vol. 1, Angus and Robertson, Sydney 1941.

Gardiner, D., *English Girlhood at School*, Oxford University Press, 1929.

Hunter, J., in Bach, J. P. S. (ed.), *An Historical Journal of Events At Sydney and at Sea*, Angus and Robertson, Sydney 1968.

Jaeger, M., *Before Victoria*, Penguin Books, Harmondsworth 1967.

Johnson, C., *Old-Time School and School Books*, Dover, New York 1963.

Johnstone, S. M., *Samuel Marsden*, Angus and Robertson, Sydney 1932.

Jones, M. G., *The Charity School Movement*, Cass, London 1964.

Kamm, J., *Hope Deferred*, Methuen, London 1965.

Kaye, F. B., (ed.), B. Mandeville, *The Fable of the Bees*, Clarendon Press, Oxford 1924.

King, J. (Rev.), *Ten Decades—the Australian Centenary Story of the London Missionary Society*, London Missionary Society, London 1895.

Lawson, J., *A Town Grammar School Through Six Centuries*, Oxford University Press, London 1963.

Macarthur, S. Onslow, (ed.), *Some Early Records of the Macarthurs of Camden*, Angus and Robertson, Sydney 1914.

Mackaness, G., *Admiral Arthur Phillip*, Angus and Robertson, Sydney 1937.

——, (ed.), *Some Letters of Rev. R. Johnson, B.A.*, 2 pts., Australian Historical Monographs, Nos 30/31, privately printed by editor, Sydney 1954.

——, (ed.), *Some Private Correspondence of the Rev. Samuel Marsden and Family*, Australian Historical Monographs, No. 4, privately printed by editor, Sydney 1942.

——, *The Life of Vice Admiral Bligh*, Angus and Robertson, Sydney 1931.

Marsden, J. B., *Life and Work of Samuel Marsden*, 2nd edn, Whitcombe and Tombs, Christchurch (N.Z.) 1913.

Mathews, H. F., *Methodism and the Education of the People 1791-1851*, The Epworth Press, London 1949.

Medlin, W., *The History of Educational Ideas in the West*, Centre for Applied Research in Education, New York 1967.

Moorehead, A., *The Fatal Impact*, Hamilton, London 1966.

Murray, L., *English Grammar*, 37th edn, Longman and others, York 1824.

O'Brien, E. M., *The Foundation of Australia*, 2nd edn, Angus and Robertson, Sydney 1950.

Penniman, H. R., (ed.), *John Locke On Politics and Education*, Van Nostrand, New York 1947.

Perry, T. M., *Australia's First Frontier*, Melbourne University Press, 1963.

Pestalozzi, J. H., *How Gertrude Teaches Her Children*, Renox House, London 1966.

Pike, D., (ed.), *Australian Dictionary of Biography, 1788-1850*, 2 cols, Melbourne University Press, 1966-7.

Price, A., *White Settlers and Native Peoples*, Georgian House, Melbourne 1950.

Reeves, C., *A History of Tasmanian Education*, Melbourne University Press, 1935.

Robson, L. L., *The Convict Settlers of Australia*, Melbourne University Press, 1965.

Rousseau, J., *Émile*, Dent, London 1957.

Shaw, A. G. L., *Convicts and the Colonies*, Faber and Faber, London 1966.

Silber, K., *Pestalozzi*, 2nd edn, Routledge and Kegan Paul, London 1965.

Smith, B., *European Vision and the South Pacific*, Clarendon Press, Oxford 1960.

Stewart, W., and McCann, W., *The Educational Innovators 1750-1880*, I, Macmillan, London 1967.

Tench, W., *Sydney's First Four Years*, Angus and Robertson, Sydney 1961.

Turney, C., (ed.), *Pioneers of Australian Education*, I, Sydney University Press, 1969.

Watts, I., *Divine Songs Attempted in Easy Language for the Use of Children*, Society for Promoting Christian Knowledge, London, n.d.

White, A. C. T., *The Story of Army Education 1643-1963*, Harrap, London 1963.

Wilson, J., *A Missionary Voyage to the Southern Pacific Ocean*, Academische Druck-u. Verdagsanstalt, London 1966.

Woolls, W., *Miscellanies in Prose and Verse*, G. Evans, Sydney 1838.

3. ARTICLES

Arndell, R., 'Ebenezer', *The N.S.W. Presbyterian*, Pts I-IV, 1964.

Bell, R., Samuel Marsden—Pioneer Pastoralist', *JRAHS*, Vol. 56, Pt. I, 1970.

Bridges, B., 'Aboriginal Education in Eastern Australia (N.S.W.) 1788-1855', *Australian Journal of Education*, Vol. 12, No. 3, October 1968.

——, 'The Aborigines and the Land Question in New South Wales, *JRAHS*, Vol. 56, Pt. 2, 1970.

Campbell, J., 'Notes on the Early History of the Glebe', *JRAHS*, Vol. XV, Pt. 5, 1929.

Connell, W., 'The Teacher in the Eighteenth and Nineteenth Centuries', *Forum of Education*, Vol. XVI, Nos 2 and 3, October 1957.

Goodin, V., 'Public Education in New South Wales before 1848', *JRAHS*, Vol. XXXVI, 4 pts., 1950.

Macnab, K., and Ward, R., 'The Nature and Nurture of the First Generation of Native-born Australians', *HSANZ*, Vol. 10, No. 39, November 1962.

McGuanne, J., 'Early Schools of New South Wales', *JRAHS*, Vol. II, Pt. IV, 1906-7.

Mulvaney, D., 'The Australian Aborigines 1606-1929', *HSANZ*, Vol. 8, No. 30, Pt. I, May 1958.

Norris, J., 'Proposals for Promoting Religion and Literature in Canada, Nova Scotia, and New Brunswick', *The Canadian Historical Review*, Vol. XXXVI, 1955.

Robinson, K., 'Population and Land Use in the Sydney District: 1788-1820', *New Zealand Geographer*, IX, 1953.

Robson, L., 'The Origin of Women Convicts Sent to Australia 1787-1852', *HSANZ*, Vol. II No. 41, November 1963.

Shellard, J., Public Education in Early New South Wales, *The Education Gazette*, Vol. LXII, Nos 2-12, 1968-9.

4. NEWSPAPERS
The Sydney Gazette, 1803-1810.

C. *Unpublished theses*

Cleverley, J., *The Administration of State Assisted Elementary Education in Mainland New South Wales 1789-1855*, PhD thesis, University of Sydney, 1967.

Gunson, W., *Evangelical Missionaries in the South Seas 1797-1860*, PhD thesis, Australian National University, 1959.

Turney, C., *The Birth of Education in Australia*, MEd thesis, University of Sydney, 1960.

INDEX